Clever with Puddings

HOME COOKING

© 1994 Time-Life Books B.V.
First published jointly by Time-Life Books B.V. and
Geddes & Grosset Ltd.

Material in this book was first published as part of the
series HEALTHY HOME COOKING.

ISBN 0 7054 2041 8

Printed in Italy.

Clever with Puddings

BY

THE EDITORS OF TIME-LIFE BOOKS

TIME-LIFE/GEDDES & GROSSET

Contents

Dessert's Eternal Role

No one needs a dessert. A fruit tart, a blackberry sorbet, a cheesecake are not likely to appear on any nutritionist's list of essential foods. Indeed, it is easy to obtain all the proteins, carbohydrates, fats and other nutrients required for a healthy diet without ever eating a dessert more complex than a slice of ripe melon. Yet for most people there would be something missing in such a regimen, an unassuaged hunger for the sweet taste, the pleasing aroma, the pretty artifice of a dessert—and the deep, abiding satisfaction it provides.

No other category of food highlights the psychological and aesthetic dimensions of eating so clearly as desserts do. The fresh tang of a strawberry-lemon sauce with strawberry halves provides its own unique delight, as does the quintessential mildness of a soothing custard. There is a gamut of textures to choose from—crunchy, creamy, dense, airy—in tantalizing combination with an even broader range of flavours. And there is diversity of temperature too—what other food can be served warm, at room temperature, chilled or frozen?

Desserts are the prime foods of festivity. What wedding or birthday would be complete without its cake, what Christmas without its pudding? Desserts, in short, make us feel good.

Controlling ingredients

The desires that desserts so abundantly fulfil can be accommodated without compromising the goal of healthy eating. The 120 desserts in this volume, which have been created and tested in the Time-Life Books kitchens, are intended to successfully round out a meal. With moderation and balance as a guide in menu planning, you can always find a place for dessert at the table— especially if you prepare the desserts as directed here and serve them in the portions recommended, which average 175 calories. Indeed, nutritionists acknowledge that refined sugar in modest quantities is not harmful to a normal person's health though its sweetness tempts us to increase intake.

The recipes in this book strive to limit sugar, honey and other sweeteners to no more than two tablespoons per serving. Of course, sugar is not the sole caloric ingredient in a dessert. Surprisingly, a teaspoon of sugar contains only 16 calories. Fats such as butter, with about 33 calories per teaspoonful, weigh in at double that amount.

The fats in desserts—usually in the form of butter, cream or egg yolks—have traditionally made pie crusts flaky, mousses smooth, custards rich. All are of animal origin however, and all contain saturated fats, which trigger a rise in the level of blood cholesterol, so strongly implicated in heart disease. But as the following recipes demonstrate, fats can be curbed without marring a dessert's appeal. Thus butter, cream and egg yolks appear in many of the recipes, but in moderate amounts— enough, certainly, to lend flavour or texture or both. Butter is generally limited to half a tablespoon (7 g) per serving; sometimes it is paired with polyunsaturated margarine to achieve flakiness in pastry without increasing saturated fat. Cream is by and large restricted to a tablespoon per portion, and a single egg yolk is divided among four servings.

Grand effects can be staged at little cost in fat. A custard can delight with fewer egg yolks than usual when the number of egg whites is increased. In many instances, low-fat, low-calorie ingredients such as yoghurt and buttermilk yield desserts that are every bit as delectable as those made with richer ingredients.

A similar stratagem can reduce the sugar in recipes. Even for some cakes, biscuits, pastries and frozen desserts, where sugar plays a crucial role, quantities can be cut without compromising taste or texture. The results are still sweet, but never cloyingly so.

Throughout this book, the emphasis is on fresh, natural ingredients bursting with good flavour. There are no artificial sweeteners, no non-dairy creamers, no imitation egg yolks. Unsweetened cocoa powder, produced by extracting fat from chocolate liquor, is used wherever it will not diminish texture and flavour. Oatmeal and nuts, strewn over a dessert as a garnish, provide protein, vitamins, minerals such as iron and phosphorus, and fibre—the carbohydrate that is believed to protect against cardiovascular disease and colon cancer. Whole-grain flours come into play, along with the more familiar white flours.

Flavour, not nutritional content, provides the incentive for including sweeteners in a dish. No sugar or syrup contains a significant amount of any nutrient. Honey, in particular, enjoys an undeserved reputation as a good source of minerals and B vitamins. However, all honeys share an attribute that makes them a valued ingredient in cakes, biscuits and pastries: they are hygroscopic, meaning they absorb water. A dessert baked with honey loses moisture more slowly and stays fresh longer than one made with another sweetener. On humid days, the honey may actually absorb moisture from the air.

The white sugars—granulated, caster and icing—have a similar taste but differ in use because of their varying textures. Brown sugars possess an earthy flavour that complements such assertive ingredients as grapefruit, raspberries and figs.

The magic of fruit

Most of the desserts in this volume derive their special identity from fruit. Fruit has many qualities to recommend it as a dessert base. It is, to begin with, inherently sweet. Natural sugar accounts for 20 per cent of the weight of a banana, and more than 60 per cent of the weight of a fresh date. For most fruits, the figure falls in the range of 10 to 15 per cent. Despite their sweetness, most fruits are low in calories: weight for weight, they contain only one fifth the calories of sugars and syrups. Using fruits is an ideal way to create desserts that satisfy the calorie limit this book seeks to maintain for individual servings.

Besides sweetness at a modest calorie count, fruits boast other advantages. They are good sources of fibre and, as a group, offer a whole alphabet of vitamins. Potassium and phosphorus are among the minerals that fruits contain, and they are remarkably low

in sodium and fat. All of this nutritional bounty is wrapped up in packages of gorgeous colours and sculptured shapes, from the pale green contours of the honeydew melon to the shiny quilted oval of the blackberry.

Many of the recipes in this book call for fresh fruits only. When a frozen substitute will work almost as well, the recipe will say so.

There are many different varieties of fruits available in the shops. No matter what the season, there should be several types available at their peak of maturity: strawberries in the spring raspberries, peaches and cherries in the summer, apples in the autumn, and oranges, lemons and grapefruit in the winter.

If you purchase fully ripe fruits, plan to use them within a day or two of their peak, for a decline in quality soon sets in. (This is especially true of berries and grapes.) Most ripe fruits—including tropical ones—should be stored in the refrigerator to retard the shift into over ripeness.

When only partially ripened fruit is available, keep it at room temperature out of direct sunlight. To speed the ripening process, pack the fruit loosely in a brown paper bag, then set the bag in a cool dry spot and fold it closed. Check the contents of the bag every day and transfer the fruits to the refrigerator as they ripen. Containers made of glass, plastic or stainless steel are best for storage—some metals can impart an unpleasant taste. Wash the fruit or wipe it clean with a damp cloth just before serving or preparing it.

Fruit's finest hours

The trick in selecting perfect fruit is to learn to recognize when it is mature, or at the peak of its developmental cycle. No fruit should be picked before it is mature; if it is, it will fail to undergo the complex chemical process of ripening, in which starches are converted into sugar, and colour, texture and flavour evolve. Most fruits will ripen properly if picked at maturity, which allow them to be shipped long distances to market without ill effect.

A few, however—notably grapes, raspberries, blackberries, strawberries, blueberries and citrus fruit—must ripen on the mother plant. The best guide to maturity is colour: if a fruit is green in whole or in part, it will not, in most cases, taste good. Again, exceptions exist—green bananas, for example will ripen properly. Some fruits, of course—greengage plums, and certain apples, pears and figs among them—are always green skinned. In judging the fitness of fruit, keep the characteristics of each type in mind. Here are some guidelines for selecting fruits:

Apricots. Avoid small, hard specimens—they are

The Key to Better Eating

Home Cooking addresses the concerns of today's weight-conscious, health-minded cooks with recipes that take into account guidelines set by nutritionists. The secret of eating well, of course, has to do with maintaining a balance of foods in the diet. The recipes thus should be used thoughtfully, in the context of a day's eating. To make the choice easier, an analysis is given of nutrients in a single serving. The counts for calories, protein, cholesterol, total fat, saturated fat, and sodium are approximate.

Interpreting the chart

The chart below gives dietary guidelines for healthy men, women and children. Recommended figures vary from country to country, but the principles are the same everywhere. The average daily amounts of calories and protein are from a report by the UK Department of Health and Social Security; the maximum advisable daily intake of fat is based on guidelines given by the National Advisory Committee on Nutrition Education (NACNE); those for cholesterol and sodium are based on upper limits suggested by the World Health Organization.

The volumes in the Home Cooking series do not purport to be diet books, nor do they focus on health foods. Rather, they express a common-sense approach to cooking that uses salt, sugar, cream, butter and oil in moderation, while employing other ingredients that also provide flavour and satisfaction. The portions themselves are modest in size.

The recipes make few unusual demands. Naturally they call for fresh ingredients, offering substitutes when these are unavailable. (The substitute is not calculated in the nutrient analysis, however.) Most of the ingredients can be found in any well-stocked supermarket.

Heavy-bottomed pots and pans are recommended to guard against burning whenever a small amount of oil is used and where there is danger of the food adhering to the hot surface, but non-stick pans can be utilized as well. Both safflower oil and virgin olive oil are favoured for sautéing. Safflower oil was chosen because it is the most highly polyunsaturated vegetable fat available in supermarkets, and polyunsaturated fats reduce blood cholesterol; if unobtainable, use sunflower oil, also high in polyunsaturated fats. Virgin olive oil is used because it has a fine fruity flavour lacking in the lesser grade known as 'pure'. In addition, it is—like all olive oil—high in monounsaturated fats, which are thought not to increase blood cholesterol. When virgin olive oil is unavailable, or when its flavour is not essential to the success of the dish, 'pure' may be used.

About cooking times

To help planning, time is taken into account in the recipes. While recognizing that everyone cooks at a different speed and that stoves and ovens differ, approximate 'working' and 'total' times are provided. Working time stands for the minutes actively spent on preparation; total time includes unattended cooking time, as well as time devoted to marinating, steeping or soaking ingredients. Since the recipes emphasize fresh foods, they may take a bit longer to prepare than 'quick and easy' dishes that call for canned or packaged products, but the difference in flavour, and often in nutrition, should compensate for the little extra time involved.

Recommended Dietary Guidelines

Average Daily Intake		Maximum Daily Intake					
		Calories	Protein grams	Cholesterol milligrams	Total fat grams	Saturated fat grams	Sodium milligrams
Females	7-8	1900	47	300	80	32	2000*
	9-11	2050	51	300	77	35	2000
	12-17	2150	53	300	81	36	2000
	18-54	2150	54	300	81	36	2000
	55-74	1900	47	300	72	32	2000
Males	7-8	1980	49	300	80	33	2000
	9-11	2280	57	300	77	38	2000
	12-14	2640	66	300	99	44	2000
	15-17	2880	72	300	108	48	2000
	18-34	2900	72	300	109	48	2000
	35-64	2750	69	300	104	35	2000
	65-74	2400	60	300	91	40	2000

* (or 5 g salt)

probably immature and will never acquire good flavour. Choose those with a lush orange colour.

Berries. Choose firm, dry berries with no trace of mould. Blackberries should be shiny and truly black, strawberries an intense, shiny red, raspberries brightly hued. Blueberries and bilberries should be veiled with a whitish, natural coating of wax called the bloom; because the bloom fades about a week after harvest, it is a sure sign of freshness. Currants should be round, plump and juicy. Red and white currants should have gleaming, translucent skins; blackcurrants should be a rich, deep colour. For most berries, size matters little. If you refrigerate such softskinned berries as raspberries for a day or so, store them in a single layer to keep bruises or mould from developing.

Cherries. Large, firm cherries are superior in flavour and texture. Look for dark shiny skins on sweet cherries.

Citrus fruits. Colour and size are not clues to flavour and juiciness. Instead, select fruits that are heavy for their size—an indication of abundant juice. Grapefruits should have thin skin; a pointed stem end suggests thick skin. Navel oranges are easier to peel and segment, but Valencia oranges contain more juice.

Figs. These delicate fruits must be picked ripe, kept under constant refrigeration and used quickly. Reject any that smell sour.

Kiwis. This fuzzy, brown, egg-shaped fruit has bright green flesh, tiny black seeds and a tangy flavour. Buy plump, firm fruit and ripen it at room temperature until its flesh yields slightly to gentle pressure.

Mangoes. There are several varieties of this sweet, fragrant fruit; the colour varies from yellow or orange to red, pink, purple or two toned. Ripen mangoes at room temperature and use them promptly.

Melons. Choose a melon that is heavy for its size. The stem end should be fragrant and yield slightly to gentle pressure. A ripe honeydew's skin is velvety rather than bald and slick.

Nectarines. Choose firm specimens with high colour and allow them to ripen at room temperature for a day or two.

Papayas. These tropical fruits have the shape of a pear and the flavour and texture of a melon. They may be either light green or pale yellow, but they ripen to a golden yellow.

Peaches. Choose fruits for their colour—creamy yellow or yellow with a red blush—and a distinctive peachy aroma.

Pears. Look for firm, clear-skinned varieties.

Pineapples. Select firm, unbruised fruit with no soft or moist spots. You can tell that a pineapple is ripe when a leaf pulled out from the centre comes away easily.

Plums. For cooking, choose a variety of plum that has a purple skin and yellow flesh. The larger, dessert plums, with red, yellow or green skins, are delicious raw but are so juicy that they paltry disintegrate when cooked.

The special uses of egg white

Another ubiquitous ingredient in this book is egg white unlike the yolk, an egg white is free of fat and cholesterol, and it contains only 16 calories. Egg white is a culinary marvel to boot, accounting for the wonderful lightness of meringues, soufflé and angel food cakes. When egg white is beaten, its elastic protein inflates in a foamy mass up to eight times its original volume.

Use uncracked eggs that have been refrigerated in their cartons. Before you break an egg, especially if you are using it raw, rinse the shell to rid it of bacteria.

Egg whites can be frozen. In fact, an angel food cake or a chiffon cake will have a better texture if it is made with thawed whites—provided the eggs were fresh when you froze them.

Beating egg whites is simple, but its success depends upon several factors. Allow the whites to come to room temperature; they will whip up faster than when chilled. Be sure that bowl, beaters, and whites contain not a speck of fat or yolk, which inhibit the formation of foam. Do not use a plastic bowl; it is virtually impossible to rid plastic of all traces of fat.

If you use a metal other than copper, or a glass or ceramic bowl, beat the egg whites until they are slightly foamy, then add a pinch of cream of tartar per white to guard against over beating. When the whites reach the desired volume, combine them the other ingredients. Do not set beaten egg whites aside for long, lest the foam begins to subside. Be sure to refrigerate desserts containing raw egg whites, and consume them within two days; bacteria can multiply rapidly in them.

The final flourish

Whatever dessert you prepare and whatever the occasion, presenting it attractively makes the eagerly awaited finale of a meal even sweeter. You may want to unmould a bombe on to a platter for all to admire before slicing it into serving portions. Glass dishes show off the radiant colours of fruits or sorbets, small bowls or plates create the pleasant optical illusion that a diner's portion is larger than it is. In serving a well-chosen dessert in the style it deserves, you will have fulfilled its timeless role bringing the meal to a happy and most satisfying conclusion.

Orange Slices Macerated in Red Wine and Port

Serves 8

Working time: about 20 minutes

Total time: about 2 hours and 20 minutes (includes chilling)

Calories 145, Protein 2g, Cholesterol 0mg, Total fat 1g, Saturated fat 1g, Sodium 2mg

6	*large oranges*
1/4 litre/8 fl oz	*Beaujolais or other fruity red wine*
4 tbsp	*sugar*
1	*cinnamon stick*
1/8 tsp	*ground cardamom or allspice*
6 tbsp	*ruby port*
2 tbsp	*currants*
2 tbsp	*toasted shredded coconut*

With a vegetable peeler, pare the rind from one of the oranges. Put the rind into a small saucepan with the wine, sugar, cinnamon stick, and cardamom or allspice.

Bring the mixture to the boil and cook it over medium-high heat until. the liquid is reduced to about 15 cl (1/4 pint)—approximately 5 minutes Remove the pan from the heat; stir in the port and currants, and set the sauce aside

Cut away the skins, removing all the white pith and slice the oranges into 5 mm (1/4 inch) thick rounds. Arrange the orange rounds on a serving dish and pour the wine sauce over them, remove and discard the cinnamon stick. Refrigerate the dish, covered, for 2 hours.

Just before serving the oranges, sprinkle the toasted coconut over all.

EDITOR'S NOTE: To toast the shredded coconut, spread it on a baking sheet and cook it in a preheated 170°C (325°F or Mark 3) oven, stirring it every 5 minutes until it has browned—about 15 minutes in all.

Poached Apricots in Caramel-Orange Sauce

Serves 8
Working time: about 45 minutes
Total time: about 2 hours and 45 minutes (includes chilling)
Calories 135, Protein 1g, Cholesterol 11mg, Total fat 3g,
Saturated fat 2g, Sodium 4mg

8	*large ripe apricots, or 16 small ripe apricots*
2.5 cm/1 inch	*length of a vanilla pod*
¼ litre/8 fl oz	*dry white wine*
200 g/7 oz	*sugar*
10 cm/4 inch	*strip of orange rind, 2.5 cm (1 inch) wide*
	fresh mint leaves for garnish
	Caramel-orange sauce
100 g/3½ oz	*sugar*
1 tsp	*fresh lemon juice*
12.5 cl/4 fl oz	*fresh orange juice*
4 tbsp	*double cream*

Blanch the apricots in boiling water for 10 seconds, then immediately transfer them to a bowl filled with iced water to arrest their cooking. Peel the apricots as soon as they are cool enough to handle. Cut open the groove in an apricot, then gently prise apart the flesh just enough to remove the stone; ease out the stone. Press the edges of the apricot closed. Repeat the process to stone the remaining apricots.

Slit the piece of vanilla pod lengthwise. In a heavy-bottomed non-reactive saucepan set over medium heat, combine the vanilla pod with ¼ litre (8 fl oz) of water, the wine, sugar and orange rind. Bring the mixture to the boil, then reduce the heat, and simmer the syrup for 5 minutes.

Reduce the heat so that the surface of the syrup barely trembles. Add the apricots and poach them, covered, until they are just tender—3 to 4 minutes. With a slotted spoon, transfer the apricots to a plate; discard the poaching syrup. Cover the apricots and chill them for 2 hours.

While the apricots are chilling, prepare the sauce. In a small, heavy-bottomed saucepan, combine the sugar with the lemon juice and 3 tablespoons of water. Bring the mixture to the boil and simmer it until it turns a reddish amber—5 to 8 minutes. Immediately remove the pan from the heat. Standing well back to avoid being splattered, slowly and carefully pour in the orange juice, then the cream. Return the pan to the stove over low heat and simmer the sauce, stirring constantly, until it thickens slightly—about 5 minutes. Pour the sauce into a small bowl; cover the bowl and refrigerate it.

To serve, spoon the chilled sauce on to individual plates and place the poached apricots in the sauce. Garnish each apricot with a mint leaf.

Orange-Banana Flowers
with Caramel Sauce

Serves 6
Working time: about 25 minutes
Total time: about 40 minutes
Calories 260, Protein 2g, Cholesterol 0mg, Total fat 1g,
Saturated fat 0g, Sodium 1mg

200 g	*sugar*
6	*oranges*
2	*large ripe bananas*
¹/₂	*lemon*

In a small, heavy saucepan, combine the sugar with 6 tablespoons of water. Bring the mixture to the boil and cook it until it turns a reddish amber. Immediately remove the pan from the heat. Standing well back to avoid being splattered, slowly and carefully pour in 4 tablespoons of water. Return the pan to the heat and simmer the sauce, stirring constantly, for 1 minute. Transfer the caramel sauce to the refrigerator to cool.

While the sauce is cooling, peel and segment the oranges as demonstrated below. Peel the bananas and slice them diagonally into pieces about 3 mm (¹/₈ inch) thick. Squeeze the lemon over the banana slices, then toss the slices to coat them with the lemon juice.

To assemble the dessert, arrange five orange segments in a circle on a plate. Place a banana slice over each of the five points where the segments meet. Arrange three orange segments in a loose circle inside the first circle, and place a banana slice over each of the three points where these segments meet. Top

the assembly with two orange segments. Quarter a banana slice and arrange the quarters on top of the last two orange segments. Assemble five more orange banana flowers in the same way.

Just before serving the flowers, pour a little caramel sauce around the outside of each one, letting some of the sauce fall on to the petals.

Segmenting a Citrus Fruit

1 TRIMMING THE ENDS. To obtain segments free of pith and membrane from a citrus fruit (here, an orange), use a sharp, stainless steel knife and slice off both ends of the fruit.

2 CUTTING THE PEEL. With the fruit standing on a flat end, slice off the peel in vertical strips, following the contour of the fruit. Rotate the fruit after each cut, and continue to remove strips until peel and pith are completely removed.

3 REMOVING THE SEGMENTS. Working over a bowl to catch the juice, hold the orange in one hand and carefully slice between flesh and membranes to free each segment. Let the segments fall into the bowl as you detach them.

Peaches with Mint and Champagne

Serves 4
Working time: about 30 minutes
Total time: about 2 hours and 30 minutes
Calories 135, Protein 1g, Cholesterol 0mg, Total fat 0g,
Saturated fat 0g, Sodium 3mg

6 *ripe peaches*
1 *orange, juice only*
1 *lime, juice only*
2 tbsp *honey*
4 tbsp *chopped fresh mint*
2.5 cl/4 fl oz *chilled dry champagne or other sparkling white wine*
1 *fresh mint sprig for garnish*
lime slices for garnish

Blanch the peaches in boiling water for 10 seconds, then drain them and run cold water over them to arrest their cooking. Peel the peaches and halve them lengthwise, discarding the stones. Thinly slice eight of the peach halves lengthwise; transfer the slices to a bowl. Put the four remaining peach halves into a food processor or a blender along with the orange juice, lime juice and honey, and purée the mixture. Blend in the chopped mint, then pour the purée over the peach slices. Cover the bowl and chill it for 2 hours.

With a slotted spoon, transfer the peaches to a serving platter. Stir the champagne into the purée remaining in the bowl, and spoon the purée over the peaches. Garnish the peaches with the mint sprig and the lime slices just before serving them.

EDITOR'S NOTE: There is no need to buy a large bottle of champagne for this recipe, small bottles are available.

Fresh Fruit in Ginger Syrup

Serves 6

Working time: about 25 minutes
Total time: about 2 hours and 30 minutes (includes chilling)
Calories 150, Protein 1g, Cholesterol 0mg, Total fat 0g,
Saturated fat 0g, Sodium 3mg

1	tart green apple, quartered, cored and cut into 1 cm (^{1}/$_2$ inch) pieces
2	ripe peaches or nectarines, halved, stoned and cut into 1 cm (^{1}/$_2$ inch) pieces
1	pear, peeled, cored and cut into 1 cm (^{1}/$_2$ inch) pieces
225 g/7 oz	blueberries, picked over and stemmed
3 tbsp	fresh lemon juice
2 tbsp	julienned orange rind
5 cm/2 inch	ginger root, cut into 5 mm (^{1}/$_4$ inch) rounds
135 g/4^1/$_2$ oz	sugar

Place the apple, peaches, pear and blueberries in a large bowl. Pour the lemon juice over the fruit and toss well, then refrigerate the bowl.

Pour 1 litre (1^3/$_4$ pints) of water into a large, heavybottomed saucepan over medium-high heat. Add the orange rind, ginger and sugar, and bring the mixture to the boil. Reduce the heat to medium and simmer the liquid until it is reduced to about ^{1}/$_2$ litre (16 fl oz) of syrup. Remove the ginger with a slotted spoon and discard it.

Pour the syrup into a large bowl and let it stand at room temperature for about 10 minutes. Add the fruit to the syrup and stir gently to coat the fruit. Refrigerate the dessert, covered, until the fruit is thoroughly chilled—about 1^1/$_2$ hours.

EDITOR'S NOTE: If blueberries are not available, bilberries, stoned cherries or seedless grapes may be used instead.

Fig Flowers with Cassis Sauce

Serves 6

Working time: about 25 minutes
Total time: about 1 hour (includes chilling)
Calories 155, Protein 1g, Cholesterol 0mg, Total fat 0g,
Saturated fat 0g, Sodium 5mg

^{1}/$_2$ litre/16 fl oz	dry white wine
1 tbsp	sugar
4 tbsp	creme de cassis
12	fresh figs
	fresh mint leaves for garnish

Combine the wine and sugar in a saucepan over medium-high heat. Cook the liquid until it is reduced to approximately 17.5 cl (6 fl oz)—about 15 minutes. Pour the reduced wine into a bowl and refrigerate it until it is cool—approximately 20 minutes. Stir the creme de cassis into the cooled liquid, then return the sauce to the refrigerator.

With a small, sharp knife, cut a cross in the top of each fig, slicing no more than half way through. Carefully cut each quarter half way down into two or three small wedges, leaving the wedges attached at the bottom; each fig will have eight to 12 wedges in all. With your fingers, press the base of the fig to spread the wedges outwards like the petals of a flower in bloom. (More cutting may be needed to separate the wedges.)

Set two fig flowers on each of six chilled dessert plates. Dribble some of the sauce over the flowers, then garnish each serving with fresh mint leaves.

Grapefruit with Grand Marnier

Serves 6
Working time: about 30 minutes
Total time: about 1 hour and 30 minutes (includes chilling)
Calories 225, Protein 2g, Cholesterol 0mg, Total fat 0g, Saturated fat 0g, Sodium 1mg

2	*limes*
2	*oranges*
2	*lemons*
4	*grapefruits*
135 g/4¹/₂ oz	*sugar*
12.5 cl/4 fl oz	*Grand Marnier or other orange-flavoured liqueur*

Use a vegetable peeler to pare strips of rind from the limes, oranges, lemons and grapefruits. Cut the strips into julienne. Halve the limes, oranges and lemons, squeeze out the juice and strain it. Pour the juice into a saucepan. Add the julienned citrus rind, the sugar, the liqueur and 6 tablespoons of water to the pan; bring the liquid to the boil. Reduce the heat and simmer the mixture until it is syrupy—about 10 minutes.

Peel the grapefruits. Working over a bowl to catch the juice, segment them. Transfer the segments and their juice to a heatproof bowl. Pour the hot syrup over the grapefruit segments and refrigerate the bowl for 1 hour before serving.

Summer Fruit Salad

Serves 6
Working time: about 25 minutes
Total time: about 1 hour and 25 minutes (includes chilling)
Calories 190, Protein 4g, Cholesterol 2g, Total fat 2g,
Saturated fat 0g, Sodium 35mg

1	watermelon (about 3 kg/6 1b), cut in half crosswise
1	lime, juice only
1	orange, juice only
90 g/3 oz	honey
300 g/10 oz	blueberries, picked over and stemmed or other berries in season
2	kiwifruits, each peeled and cut into 8 pieces
¹/₄ litre	plain low-fat yoghurt
2 tbsp	Grand Marnier or other orange-flavoured liqueur.

With a melon baller, scoop the watermelon flesh from the shell. Set the watermelon balls aside. (If you do not have a melon baller, remove the flesh with a curved grapefruit knife and cut it into uniform cubes, discarding the seeds.) Scrape out and discard any remaining flesh. Notch the rim of one shell half with a decorative zigzag and refrigerate the shell. Discard the other half.

To make the dressing, combine the lime juice, orange juice and half of the honey in a large bowl. Add to the dressing the watermelon balls, blueberries and kiwi fruits. Toss the fruit well, then refrigerate the salad for 1 hour.

To prepare the sauce, whisk together the yoghurt, the remaining 2 tablespoons of honey and the liqueur. Refrigerate the sauce.

At serving time, set the watermelon shell on a large platter. Toss the salad once more to coat the fruit with the dressing, then spoon the fruit into the watermelon shell. Serve the chilled sauce in a separate bowl.

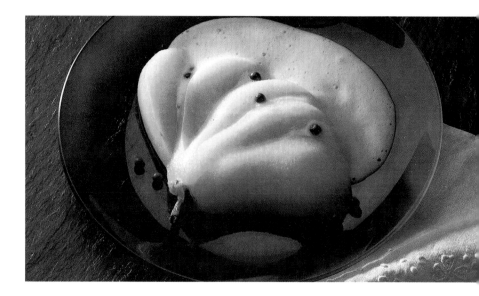

Peppercorn Pears in Sabayon Sauce

Serves 8
Working time: about 1 hour
Total time: about 2 hours (includes chilling)
Calories 180, Protein 2g, Cholesterol 70mg, Total fat 2g,
Saturated fat 0g, Sodium 19mg

1	*lemon halved*
4	*firm but ripe pears*
200 g/7 oz	*sugar*
1/4 litre/8 fl oz	*dry white wine*
8	*black peppercorns*
2	*eggs*
1/2 tsp	*pure vanilla extract*
1 tbsp	*brine-packed green peppercorns, drained*

Prepare acidulated water by squeezing the juice from one of the lemon halves into 1 litre (1³/₄ pints) of cold water. Peel, halve, and core the pears, dropping them into the acidulated water to prevent them from discolouring as you work.

In a large, shallow, non-reactive pan, combine the sugar, ¹/₄ litre (8 fl oz) of water, the wine and the black peppercorns Pare a strip of lemon rind from the reserved lemon half and add it to the pan. Squeeze the juice of the remaining lemon half into the pan as well. Bring the liquid to the boil, then reduce the heat to low, and simmer the mixture for 5 minutes

Transfer the pears to the sugar syrup and poach them in a single layer for about 3 minutes on each side. With a slotted spoon, transfer the pears to a plate.

Continue to simmer the poaching liquid over low heat until it is reduced to about ¹/₄ litre (8 fl oz) of heavy syrup—5 to 10 minutes. Remove the peppercorns and rind with a spoon. Reserve 6 tablespoons of the syrup, pour the remainder over the pears, cover them and refrigerate them until they are chilled—about 1 hour.

Let the reserved syrup cool for 5 minutes, then use it to prepare the sabayon sauce. Whisk the eggs in a small, heavy-bottomed saucepan. Pour the syrup into the pan in a thin, steady stream, whisking constantly so that its heat does not curdle the eggs. Cook the mixture over medium heat, stirring constantly until it coats the back of the spoon—3 to 4 minutes. Transfer the custard to a bowl. With an electric mixer set on high, whip the sauce until it has quadrupled in volume and is cool—about 5 minutes. Blend in the vanilla extract, then refrigerate the sabayon sauce, covered, until it is chilled—about 1 hour.

When the pears are chilled, cut them into fans: set a pear half core side down on the work surface. Holding the knife at a 45-degree angle to the work surface, cut the pear half into five lengthwise slices, leaving the slices attached at the stem end. Gently transfer the pear half to a dessert plate, then spread out the slices in the shape of a fan. Repeat the process to make eight fans in all. Spoon about 1 tablespoon of the chilled sabayon sauce next to each portion. Sprinkle each fan with a few green peppercorns and serve at once.

Plums with Cream

Serves 6

Working time: about 20 minutes

Total time: about 1 hour and 15 minutes (includes chilling)

Calories 135, Protein 1g, Cholesterol 9mg, Total fat 3g,
Saturated fat 2g, Sodium 8mg

750 g/1¹/₂ lb	*ripe purple plums, halved and stoned*
4 tbsp	*sugar*
3 tbsp	*arrowroot, mixed with ¹/₄ litre (8 fl oz) water*
6 tbsp	*single cream*

Combine the plums, sugar and the arrowroot mixture in a large, heavy-bottomed saucepan. Bring the plum mixture to a simmer over medium heat, stirring constantly. Reduce the heat to maintain a slow simmer and cover the pan. Cook the plums, stirring them from time to time, until they become very soft—about 20 minutes.

Transfer the plums to a food processor or a blender, and purée them. Strain the purée through a sieve into a large bowl. Ladle the purée into six small serving bowls. Cover the bowls and chill them for at least 30 minutes. Spoon 2 tablespoons of the cream over each portion and serve.

Strawberries with Lemon-Strawberry Sauce

Serves 8

Working (and total) time: about 45 minutes

Calories 155, Protein 2g, Cholesterol 70mg, Total fat 2g,
Saturated fat 0g, Sodium 19mg

2	*eggs*
175 g/6 oz	*caster sugar*
4 tbsp	*cornflour*
2	*lemons, grated rind only*
12.5 cl/4 fl oz	*fresh lemon juice*
1 kg/2 lb	*strawberries, hulled and halved carambola (star fruit), thinly sliced (optional)*

In a heavy-bottomed saucepan, whisk together the eggs and the sugar; then mix in the cornflour, lemon rind, lemon juice and 12.5 cl (4 fl oz) of water. Set the lemon mixture over medium heat and stir it continuously until it comes to the boil. Continue cooking and stirring the mixture until it is quite thick—about 2 minutes more. Set the mixture aside to cool.

Purée 150 g (5 oz) of the strawberries in a food processor or blender. Mix the lemon mixture into the purée. To serve, spoon some of the lemon-strawberry sauce into eight dessert glasses or bowls. Carefully set the remaining strawberries in the sauce; garnish each serving, if you like, with carambola slices.

Apple-Prune Timbales with Lemon Syrup

Serves 6

Working time: about 40 minutes

Total time: about 1 hour and 10 minutes

Calories 140, Protein 1g, Cholesterol 5mg, Total fat 2g, Saturated fat 1g, Sodium 2mg

15 g/¹/₂ oz	*unsalted butter*
850 g/1³/₄ lb	*tart green apples, peeled, cored and cut into 1 cm (¹/₂ inch) pieces*
¹/₂ tsp	*ground coriander*
¹/₈ tsp	*ground cloves*
2 tbsp	*fresh lemon juice*
4 tbsp	*brandy*
125 g/4 oz	*stoned prunes, quartered*
60 g/2 oz	*sultanas*
4 tbsp	*sugar*
1	*lemon, rind only, finely julienned*

Melt the butter in a large, heavy sauté pan over medium-high heat Add the apple pieces, coriander and cloves, and cook the mixture, stirring constantly, for 5 minutes. Stir in the lemon juice, brandy, prunes, sultanas, 3 tablespoons of the sugar and 12.5 cl (4 fl oz) of water. Cook the compote, stirring frequently, until nearly all the liquid has evaporated—about 10 minutes.

While the apple compote is cooking, combine the rind, the remaining tablespoon of sugar and 4 tablespoons of water in a small saucepan. Bring the mixture to the boil, then reduce the heat to low; simmer the mixture until the liquid is thick and syrupy—about 7 minutes.

Spoon the apple compote into six 12.5 cl (4 fl oz) ramekins, tamping it down in order to give the timbales a uniform shape when they are unmoulded. Let the ramekins stand at room temperature until tepid— approximately 30 minutes.

Unmould the timbales on to individual plates. Garnish each with some of the lemon rind and dribble the lemon syrup over the top.

20

Bring the sauce to the boil, then reduce the heat, and simmer the mixture, stirring occasionally, until it is reduced by half—about 15 minutes, (There should be about 4 tablespoons of thick sauce.) Stir in the kirsch and the vanilla extract, then pour the sauce over the cherries. Grill the cherries for 2 to 3 minutes. Serve the cherries hot, with a spoonful of sauce dribbled over each portion.

Stoning a Cherry

1 INSERTING THE BLADE. Grip a swivel-bladed vegetable peeler on either side of the blade, avoiding the cutting edges. Insert the tip into the top of a cherry from which the stem has been removed, and work the peeler's curved tip round the stone.

Black Forest Cherries

Serves 4

Working (and total) time: about 30 minutes

Calories 225, Protein 2g, Cholesterol 20mg, Total fat 7g, Saturated fat 4g, Sodium 75mg

500 g/1 lb	*sweet cherries*
4 tbsp	*sugar*
1 tbsp	*unsweetened cocoa powder*
1/8 tsp	*salt*
4 tbsp	*double cream*
4 tbsp	*kirsch*
1/2 tsp	*pure vanilla extract*

Stone the cherries as shown on the right.

Combine 4 tablespoons of water with the sugar in a heavy saucepan set over medium-high heat, and bring the mixture to the boil. Add the cherries and stir gently to coat them with the syrup. Cook the cherries for 1 minute. Using a slotted spoon, transfer the poached cherries to a gratin dish or other fireproof serving dish, and set the dish aside. Remove the saucepan with the syrup from the heat.

Preheat the grill.

In a bowl, combine the cocoa and salt. Pouring in a steady stream, whisk the cream into the cocoa and salt. Stir the mixture into the syrup in the saucepan.

2 REMOVING THE STONE. Wriggle the tip of the peeler back and forth to loosen the stone from the surrounding flesh. Then prise the stone up through the top of the fruit to dislodge it.

Poached Peaches
with Berry Sauce

Serves 8
Working time about 30 minutes
Total time: about 2 hours and 30 minutes (includes chilling)
Calories 120, Protein 1g, Cholesterol 10mg, Total fat 3g,
Saturated fat 2g, Sodium 4 mg

8	*firm but ripe peaches*
1/2 litre/16 fl oz	*dry white wine*
200 g/7 oz	*sugar*
5 cm/2 inch	*strip of lemon rind*
8	*mints sprigs (optional)*
	Berry sauce
175g/6 oz	*fresh or frozen black berries or*
	raspberries
2 tbsp	*caster sugar*
4 tbsp	*double cream*

Blanch the peaches in boiling water until their skins loosen—30 seconds to 1 minute. Remove the peaches and run cold water over them to arrest the cooking.

When the peaches are cool enough to handle, peel them and cut them in half lengthwise, discarding the stones.

Put the wine, sugar and lemon rind into a large saucepan. Bring the liquid to the boil, then reduce the heat and simmer the mixture for 5 minutes. Add the peach halves to the liquid and poach them until they are just tender—3 to 5 minutes. Using a slotted spoon, transfer the peach halves to a plate. Discard the poaching syrup. Cover the plate and refrigerate it for at least 2 hours.

To make the berry sauce, purée 125 g (4 oz) of the berries with the caster sugar in a food processor or a blender, then strain the purée through a fine sieve into a jug or bowl. Stir the cream into the purée.

To serve, arrange two peach halves on each of eight dessert plates and pour a little of the berry sauce over each portion. Garnish each serving with a few of the remaining berries and, if you like, a sprig of mint.

Rum-Soused Plantains with Oranges and Kiwi Fruits

Serves 6

Working (and total) time: about 45 minutes

Calories 200, Protein 1g, Cholesterol 10mg, Total fat 4g,
Saturated fat 2g, Sodium 4mg

2	oranges
4 tbsp	caster sugar
30 g/1 oz	unsalted butter
2	larger ripe plantains, peeled and sliced diagonally into 1 cm (½ inch) pieces
6 tbsp	dark rum
2	ripe kiwi fruit
1 tbsp	icing sugar

Squeeze the juice from one of the oranges. Strain the juice into a small bowl and whisk the caster sugar into it. Set the bowl aside. Peel the second orange; working over another bowl to catch the juice, segment the second orange. Set the segments aside. Strain the juice in the second bowl into the sweetened juice.

Melt the butter in a large, heavy frying pan over medium-high heat. Add the plantain slices and cook them for 2 minutes. Turn the plantains over and cook them on the second side for 2 minutes.

Pour the orange juice over the plantains and continue cooking them until the liquid reaches a simmer. Cook the plantains at a simmer for 2 minutes. Pour all but 1 tablespoon of the rum over the plantains. Turn the plantains over and continue cooking them until they are soft—2 to 4 minutes more.

Remove the pan from the heat; with a slotted spoon, transfer the plantain slices to a fireproof baking dish. Reserve the liquid in the pan. Arrange the plantain slices in the dish, inserting the orange segments among them.

Peel and chop one of the kiwi fruits, and press it through a sieve into the liquid in the pan . Stir the sieved fruit into the liquid, then pour the liquid over the plantain slices and orange segments. Peel, quarter, and slice the other kiwi fruit; set the slices aside.

Sprinkle the icing sugar over the contents of the baking dish, set the dish below a preheated grill just long enough to melt the sugar. Garnish the dish with the kiwi slices. Dribble the remaining tablespoon of rum over all and serve immediately.

Blackberry-Peach Crumble

Serves 8

Working time: about 30 minutes
Total time: about 1 hour and 15 minutes
Calories 175, Protein 3g, Cholesterol 30mg, Total fat 3g,
Saturated fat 1g, Sodium 200mg

6	ripe peaches
1 tbsp	fresh lemon juice
4 tbsp	sugar
500 g/1 lb	blackberries, picked over and stemmed, or other berries in season

Crumble topping

90 g/3 oz	wholemeal flour
1 tsp	baking powder
$^1/_4$ tsp	salt
15 g/$^1/_2$ oz	cold unsalted butter
125 g/4 oz	caster sugar
1	egg
$^1/_2$ tsp	ground cinnamon
1 tbsp	wheat germ

Preheat the oven to 190°C (375°F or Mark 5).

Blanch the peaches in boiling water until their skins loosen—30 seconds to 1 minute. Peel the peaches and halve them lengthwise, discarding the stones. Cut each peach half into five or six slices. Put the slices in a bowl, add the lemon juice and sugar, and gently toss them together. Set aside.

To prepare the crumble topping, put the flour, baking powder, salt, butter and 100 g ($3^1/_2$ oz) of the sugar into a food processor; mix the ingredients just long enough to produce a fine-meal texture. Alternatively, put the dry ingredients into a bowl and cut the butter in using a pastry blender or two knives. Add the egg and blend it in—5 to 10 seconds. The topping should have the texture of large crumbs.

Arrange the peach slices in an even layer in a large, shallow baking dish. Scatter the blackberries over the peach slices, then sprinkle the topping over the blackberries. Stir together the cinnamon, wheat germ and the remaining sugar, and strew this mixture over the crumble topping. Bake the dish until the topping is brown and the juices bubble up around the edges—45 to 55 minutes.

EDITOR'S NOTE: For added fibre, leave the peach skins on.

Strawberry Blossoms with Pears and Red Wine Sauce

Serves 8

Working (and total) time: about 45 minutes

Calories 225, Protein 1g, Cholesterol 4mg, Total fat 3g,
Saturated fat 1g, Sodium 5mg

60 cl/1 pint	red wine
135 g/4$^{1}/_{2}$ oz	sugar
1.5 kg/3 lb	firm, ripe pears, peeled, quartered and cored
15 g/$^{1}/_{2}$ oz	unsalted butter
2 tbsp	fresh lemon juice
750 g/1$^{1}/_{2}$ lb	strawberries, hulled

Combine the wine and half of the sugar in a heavy saucepan over medium heat. Cook the wine, stirring occasionally, until it is reduced to about $^{1}/_{4}$ litre (8 fl oz)—about 30 minutes. Transfer the sauce to a bowl and refrigerate it until it is cool.

While the wine is reducing, cut the pears into thin strips. Melt the butter in a large, shallow, heavy-bot-tomed pan over medium heat. Add the pears, lemon juice and the remaining sugar; cook the mixture, stir-ring frequently, until almost all the liquid has evapo-rated—15 to 20 minutes. Transfer the pear mixture to a plate and refrigerate it until it is cool.

Set eight of the smaller berries aside. Stand the re-maining strawberries on a cutting board and cut them into vertical slices about 3 mm ($^{1}/_{8}$ inch) thick.

Spoon about 4 tablespoons of the chilled pear mix-ture into the centre of a large dessert plate. Arrange some of the larger strawberry slices in a ring inside the pear mixture, overlapping the slices and propping them at a slight angle to resemble the petals of a flower. Form a smaller ring of strawberry slices inside the first and stand a whole berry in the centre. Repeat the proc-ess with the remaining pear mixture and strawberries to form eight portions in all.

Just before serving, pour a little of the red wine sauce round the outside of each blossom, letting a few drops fall on to the petals themselves.

Tropical Fruit
Compote with Rum

Serves 8
Working time: about 30 minutes
Total time: about 2 hours and 30 minutes (includes chilling)
Calories 187, Protein 1g, Cholesterol 0mg, Total fat 1g,
Saturated fat 0g, Sodium 2mg

100 g/3¹/₂ oz *sugar*
2 tbsp *fresh lime juice*
1 *strip of lime rind*
1 *pineapple, peeled, sliced into 8 rounds and cored*
2 *mangoes, each cut into 8 wedges and peeled (opposite)*
3 *bananas, peeled, each cut diagonally into 8 pieces*
6 tbsp *white rum*
1 *fresh mint sprig (optional)*

In a small saucepan, combine 17.5 cl (6 fl oz) of water with the sugar, lime juice and lime rind. Bring the liquid to the boil, then reduce the heat, and simmer the mixture for 5 minutes. Pour the syrup into a bowl; remove the lime rind and chill the syrup for about 2 hours.

To serve the compote, arrange the fruit on a serving plate. Stir the rum into the chilled syrup, then pour just enough of the liquid over the fruit to moisten it. If you like, garnish the fruit with a sprig of mint. Serve the remaining syrup in a sauceboat.

Peeling and Slicing a Pineapple

1 REMOVING THE TOP. With a sharp, stainless steel knife (here, a medium-sized chef's knife,), slice off the pineapple's bushy green top. Turn the fruit round and slice off 2.5 cm (1 inch) or so from the bottom.

2 REMOVING THE SKIN. Stand the pineapple on end and slice off a strip of skin, following the contour of the fruit. Cut deep enough to remove most of the dark eyes Continue slicing until all the skin is removed

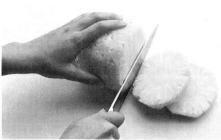

3 CUTTING SLICES. Cut out any of the eyes that remain. Place the fruit on its side and, steadying it with one hard hand divide the pineapple into as many slices as the recipe calls for.

4 CORING THE SLICES. With a small biscuit cutter, as is shown here, or an apple corer, firmly stamp out and discard the tough, fibrous centre of each pineapple slice. If you do not have a small cutter or a corer, remove the centre with the tip of a paring knife.

Preparing a Mango

1 REMOVING THE PEEL. Cut a thin slice frim the mango's stem side. Hold the fruit, stem side up, in the palm of one hand, and use a paring or utility knife to peel the skin from the flesh, starting each cut from the exposed end.

2 CUTTING AWAY THE HALVES. Stand the mango upright on its flat end and slice down one side—following the contour of the large, oval stone—to free one half of the fruit. Cut along the other side of the stone to remove the other half of the mango.

3 SLICING UP THE HALVES. Lay a half cut side down on the cutting board. Cut the fruit in half lengthwise, then slice each piece in half, then slice each half again to obtain the wedges called in for the recipe on page 26. (To obtain mango cubes, cut up the wedges and the flesh remaining on the stone.)

Pineapple Gratin

Serves 6

Working time: about 20 minutes

Total time: about 30 minutes

Calories 170, Protein 2g, Cholesterol 45mg, Total fat 1g,
Saturated fat 0g, Sodium 20mg

1	*large ripe pineapple*
2 tbsp	*raisins*
2 tbsp	*sultanas*
5 tbsp	*pure maple syrup*
3 tbsp	*bourbon or white rum*
1	*egg yolk*
$^{1}/_{2}$ tsp	*pure vanilla extract*
$^{1}/_{4}$ tsp	*ground ginger*
1 tbsp	*cornflour*
2	*egg whites, at room temperature*
2 tbsp	*dark brown sugar*

Preheat the oven to 240°C (475°F or Mark 9).

Trim and peel the pineapple as demonstrated in steps 1 and 2 on page 28. Stand the pineapple upright and cut it in half from top to bottom. Remove the core from each half by cutting a shallow V-shaped groove down the centre, then cut each half crosswise into nine slices.

Overlap the pineapple slices in a large, shallow baking dish. Scatter the raisins and sultanas over the pineapple slices. Dribble 2 tablespoons of the maple syrup over the top, then sprinkle the dish with 2 tablespoons of the bourbon or rum. Cover the dish and set it aside at room temperature.

In a small bowl, blend the egg yolk with the vanilla extract, ginger, cornflour, the remaining maple syrup and the remaining bourbon or rum. In a separate bowl, beat the two egg whites until they form soft peaks. Stir half of the beaten egg whites into the yolk mixture to lighten it. Gently fold the yolk mixture into the remaining beaten egg whites.

Bake the dish containing the pineapple until the slices are heated through—about 3 minutes. Remove the dish from the oven and spread the egg mixture evenly over the top of the egg mixture. Rub the sugar through a sieve over the fruit. Return the dish to the oven and bake the pineapple until the sugar melts and the topping browns and puffs up slightly—about 5 minutes. Serve the gratin immediately.

Baked Plums
with Streusel Topping

Serves 8
Working time: about 30 minutes
Total time: about 45 minutes
Calories 185, Protein 2g, Cholesterol 8mg, Total fat 6g,
Saturated fat 2g, Sodium 5mg

8 *ripe purple plums, quartered and stoned*
¼ litre/8 fl oz *brandy*
4 tbsp *dark brown sugar*
1 *orange, grated rind only*
Streusel topping
4 tbsp *oatmeal*
4 tbsp *plain flour*
30 g/1 oz *unsalted butter, softened*
5 tbsp *dark brown sugar*
4 tbsp *finely chopped walnuts*
1 *orange, grated rind only*

Arrange the plum quarters skin side up in a 20 cm (8 inch) square baking dish. Preheat the oven to 200°C (400°F or Mark 6).

Combine the brandy, brown sugar and orange rind a small saucepan. Bring the mixture to the boil, then cook it until the liquid is reduced to 4 tablespoons—about 5 minutes. Pour the brandy syrup evenly over the plums.

To make the streusel topping, chop the oatmeal in a food processor or a blender until it is as fine as flour. Transfer the chopped oatmeal to a large bowl and mix in the flour, butter, brown sugar, walnuts and rind. Dot the surface of the plums with spoonfuls of the topping. Bake the plums until the streusel has browned and the fruit juices are bubbling—15 to 20 minutes.

Mixed Berry Cobbler

Serves 8
Working (and total) time: about 30 minutes
Calories 180, Protein 2g, Cholesterol 10mg, Total fat 6g,
Saturated fat 3g, Sodium 5mg

250 g/8 oz *fresh or frozen raspberries, thawed*
300 g/10 oz *fresh or frozen blackberries, thawed*
300 g/10 oz *fresh or frozen blueberries, thawed, or*
other berries
4 tbsp *fresh lemon juice*
4 tbsp *sugar*

Oatmeal topping

100 g/3¹/₂ oz *rolled oats*
4 tbsp *dark brown sugar*
45 g/1¹/₂ oz *unsalted butter*

Preheat the oven to 180°C (350°F or Mark 4)

To prepare the topping, combine the oats and brown sugar in a small bowl. Spread the mixture in a baking tin and bake it until it turns light brown—8 to 10 minutes. Cut the butter into small pieces and scatter them in the tin. Return the tin to the oven until the butter has melted—about 1 minute. Stir the oats to coat them with the butter and bake the mixture for 5 minutes more. Set the oatmeal topping aside to cool. (The topping may be made ahead and stored, tightly covered, for several days.)

Put half of each of the berries into a large bowl and set them aside. Combine the lemon juice with the sugar in a saucepan and bring the mixture to the boil. Add the remaining blueberries to the syrup; reduce the heat to low and cook the fruit for 3 minutes. Add the remaining raspberries along with the remaining blackberries. Bring the mixture to a simmer and cook it, stirring constantly, for 3 minutes. Pour the cooked fruit into a sieve set over the bowl of reserved berries, use the back of a wooden spoon to press the fruit through the sieve. Stir gently to coat the whole berries with the sauce.

To serve, spoon the warm fruit mixture into individual ramekins or small bowls. Sprinkle some of the topping over each portion.

EDITOR'S NOTE: If you prefer not to add the oatmeal topping, the fruit mixture may be served on its own, or it may be spooned over frozen yoghurt.

Pear and Cranberry Crisp

Serves 8

Working time: about 30 minutes

Total time: about 1 hour and 10 minutes

Calories 190, Protein 3g, Cholesterol 8mg, Total fat 5g,
Saturated fat 2g, Sodium 2mg

1	*lemon*
200 g/7 oz	*fresh or frozen cranberries*
6 tbsp	*sugar*
4	*pears*

Oat topping

140 g/4^1/$_2$ oz	*rolled oats*
4 tbsp	*unsweetened apple juice*
30 g/1 oz	*unsalted butter, melted*

With a vegetable peeler, pare the rind from the lemon. Chop the rind finely and set it aside. Squeeze the lemon, straining and reserving the juice.

Combine the cranberries with 4 tablespoons of the sugar, the lemon rind and 4 tablespoons of water in a saucepan over medium-high heat. Bring the mixture to the boil and cook it, stirring occasionally, until berries burst—about 10 minutes. Set aside.

Peel and core the pears, then coarsely chop them.

Transfer the pears to a heavy-bottomed saucepan. Dribble the lemon juice over the pears and bring the mixture to the boil. Reduce the heat to maintain a simmer, then cook the mixture, stirring occasionally, until the pears reach the consistency of thick apple sauce—20 to 30 minutes. Set the pears aside.

Preheat the oven to 200°C (400°F or Mark 6).

For the topping, mix together the oats, apple juice and butter. Spread the oat mixture on a baking sheet and bake it, stirring occasionally, until it has browned—20 to 30 minutes. Remove the topping from the oven and reduce the temperature to 180°C (350°F or Mark 4).

Spread about 2 tablespoons of the oat mixture in the bottom of a lightly oiled 1.5 litre (2^1/$_2$ pint) baking dish. Spread half of the pear mixture in the dish, then top it with half of the cranberry mixture in an even layer. Spread half of the remaining oat topping over the cranberry mixture. Repeat the layering process with the remaining pear, cranberry and oat mixtures to fill the dish . Sprinkle the remaining 2 tablespoons of sugar on top. Bake the crisp until the juices are bubbling hot in the centre—20 to 30 minutes.

Ricotta-Stuffed Pears in Apricot Sauce

Serves 4

Working time: about 30 minutes

Total time: about 1 hour and 15 minutes

Calories 315, Protein 5g, Cholesterol 10mg, Total fat 4g,
Saturated fat 1g, Sodium 45mg

¹/₂ litre/16 fl oz	*dry white wine*
125 g/4 oz	*sugar*
4	*large firm but ripe pears*
¹/₂	*lemon*
150 g/5 oz	*fresh dried apricots or 60 g (2 oz) dried apricots*
125 g/4 oz	*low-fat ricotta cheese*
15 g/¹/₂ oz	*plain chocolate finely chopped*
4	*chocolate leaves (optional)*

Combine the wine, 100 g (3¹/₂ oz) of the sugar and ¹/₂ litre (16 fl oz) of water in a large saucepan over medium heat. Bring the liquid to a simmer.

Meanwhile, peel the pears, leaving their stems attached; as you work, lightly rub the cut lemon half over the pears to keep them from discolouring. Using a melon baller or a small spoon, core the pears from the bottom. Squeeze the lemon half into the saucepan, then add the lemon shell to the liquid

Carefully lower the pears into the simmering liquid Poach the pears, turning them after 5 minutes, until they are somewhat translucent—about 10 minutes in all. While the pears are cooking, prepare the apricots If you are using fresh apricots, blanch them in boiling water for 30 seconds to 1 minute to loosen their skins then run cold water over the apricots to arrest their cooking. Peel and stone them. Whether you are using fresh or dried apricots, coarsely chop them.

Remove the pears from the poaching liquid with a slotted spoon and set them upright on a plate to drain. Refrigerate the pears. Reserve 1/2 litre (16 fl oz) of the liquid and discard the rest.

Add all but 2 tablespoons of the chopped apricots to the poaching liquid. Continue simmering the liquid until it is reduced to approximately 17.5 cl (6 fl oz)—about 15 minutes. Purée the apricots and the liquid in a food processor or a blender. Refrigerate the purée.

While the poaching liquid is reducing, mix together the ricotta, the chocolate and the remaining sugar. Finely chop the reserved 2 tablespoons of chopped apricots and stir them in. Put the ricotta mixture into the refrigerator to chill.

To serve, fill each pear with one quarter of the chilled ricotta mixture. Pour some of the apricot purée on to each of four plates; set a stuffed pear in the centre and garnish the stem end with a chocolate leaf if you wish.

Chocolate Leaves

Makes 8 leaves
Working time: about 20 minutes
Total time: about 1 hour
Per leaf: Calories 18, Protein 0g, Cholesterol 0mg, Total fat 1g, Saturated fat 1g, Sodium 0mg

30 g/1 oz *plain chocolate, chopped*

Carefully wash, rinse and dry eight rose leaves, and set them aside. Put the chocolate into a ramekin or a cup. Fill a saucepan 2.5 cm (1 inch) deep with water and set the ramekin or cup in it; bring the water to a simmer. As soon as the chocolate has melted, use a small, clean paint brush or other small brush to coat one side of a rose leaf with a generous amount of chocolate as demonstrated on the right. Set the painted leaf, chocolate side up, on a chilled tray or plate to cool. Coat the remaining leaves, then put the tray or plate into the freezer until the chocolate hardens—about 5 minutes.

Remove the chocolate leaves from the freezer. Working rapidly from the stem end, peel back a green leaf to separate it from the chocolate leaf. Return the chocolate leaf to the chilled tray. Repeat the process to separate the remaining leaves. Store the chocolate leaves in the refrigerator or freezer until shortly before use; they melt rapidly if the temperature of the room is warm.

EDITOR'S NOTE: Leftover chocolate can be stored in an airtight container and reserved for another use.

Making Chocolate Leaves

1 APPLYING THE CHOCOLATE. Melt chocolate as directed in the recipe. With a small, clean brush, thickly paint one surface of a clean rose leaf. Set the leaf chocolate side up. on a chilled tray. Coat all the leaves, then cool them in the freezer for at least 5 minutes.

2 PEELING THE LEAF. When the chocolate has hardened, remove the tray from the freezer. Working rapidly, gently pull the chocolate and rose leaves apart from stem to tip. Refrigerate the chocolate leaves until you are ready to use them.

Nectarine Cobbler

Serves 8

Working time: about 30 minutes
Total time: about 1 hour and 20 minutes
Calories 285, Protein 6g, Cholesterol 40mg, Total fat 4g,
Saturated fat 2g, Sodium 175mg

8 *large ripe nectarines*
6 tbsp *light brown sugar*
$^1/_2$ tsp *ground cinnamon*
$^1/_2$ tsp *grated nutmeg*
1 tbsp *fresh lemon juice*
2 tbsp *caster sugar*

Cake topping

215 g/7$^1/_2$ oz *plain flour*
1$^1/_2$ tsp *baking powder*
$^1/_4$ tsp *salt*

100 g/3$^1/_2$ oz *caster sugar*
15 g/$^1/_2$ oz *cold unsalted butter*
17.5 cl/6 fl oz *semi-skimmed milk*
1 tsp *pure vanilla extract*

Preheat the oven to 190°C (375° F or Mark 5). Halve the nectarines lengthwise, discarding the stones. Thinly slice the nectarine halves lengthwise. In a bowl, gently toss the slices with the brown sugar, cinnamon, nutmeg and lemon juice. Transfer the contents of the bowl to a large, shallow baking dish and spread out the nectarine slices in an even layer.

For the cake topping, sift the flour, baking powder, salt and caster sugar into a bowl. Cut in the butter with a pastry blender or two knives, blending the mixture just long enough to give it a fine-meal texture. In a separate bowl, mix together the egg, milk and vanilla extract, then pour this mixture into the bowl containing the flour. Using a fork, stir the mixture briskly just until it is well blended—about 30 seconds.

Dot the nectarine slices with evenly spaced spoonfuls of the topping, then smooth the topping so that it covers the fruit. Bake the cobbler for 20 minutes, then sprinkle the 2 tablespoons of sugar over the top. Continue baking the cobbler until the topping is brown, puffed and firm, and the juices bubble up around the edges—20 to 30 minutes more.

Pears with Hazelnuts

Serves 4
Working time: about 30 minutes
Total time: about 45 minutes
Calories 225, Protein 2g, Cholesterol 8mg, Total fat 8g, Saturated fat 2g, Sodium 5mg

30 g/1 oz *shelled hazelnuts*
4 tbsp *light brown sugar*
15 g/¹/₂ oz *cold unsalted butter*
4 *large ripe pears*
¹/₂ *lemon*
1 tbsp *fresh lemon juice*

Preheat the oven to 190°C (375°F or Mark 5).

Spread the nuts in a single layer in a small cake tin or a roasting pan. Toast the nuts in the oven for 10 minutes. Test a nut for doneness by rubbing it in a clean tea towel; the skin should come off easily. (If it does not, toast the nuts for 2 minutes more and repeat the test.) When the nuts are done, wrap them in the towel and rub off their skins. Let the nuts cool to room temperature.

Put the nuts, brown sugar and butter into a food processor or a blender, and process them just until the nuts are coarsely chopped. Set the mixture aside.

Preheat the grill. Peel the pears, then halve them lengthwise, and core them, rubbing them with the lemon half as you work to prevent discoloration. Arrange the pear halves, cored sides up, in a large, shallow baking dish. Moisten the pears with the lemon juice and sprinkle the nut mixture over them. Grill the pears until the topping browns and bubbles—about 2 minutes.

Apple Brown Betty
with Cheddar Cheese

Serves 6

Working time: about 30 minutes

Total time: about 1 hour and 15 minutes

Calories 255, Protein 5g, Cholesterol 11mg, Total fat 4g,
Saturated fat 2g, Sodium 170mg

6	*firm wholemeal bread slices, crusts removed*
6	*large tart green apples*
125 g/4 oz	*caster sugar*
1/2 tsp	*ground cinnamon*
1 tbsp	*fresh lemon juice*
12.5 cl/4 fl oz	*unsweetened apple juice*
60 g/2 oz	*mature Cheddar cheese, grated*

Preheat the oven to 150°C (300°F or Mark 2). Cut the bread slices into 1 cm (1/2 inch) cubes and spread them out on a baking sheet. Bake the bread cubes for 10 minutes, stirring them once to ensure that they cook evenly without browning. Remove the bread cubes from the oven and set them aside. Increase the oven temperature to 190°C (375°F or Mark 5).

Peel, quarter and core the apples, then cut the quarters into thin slices. In a bowl, gently toss the slices with 100 g (3 1/2 oz) of the sugar, the cinnamon, lemon juice and apple juice. Spoon half of the apple mixture into a 1.5 litre (2 1/2 pint) baking dish. Cover the apple mixture with half of the toasted bread cubes. Form another layer with the remaining apple mixture and then the bread cubes. Scatter the grated Cheddar cheese over the bread cubes and sprinkle the remaining sugar evenly over the top.

Bake the dish until the juices bubble up around the edges and the top browns—about 45 minutes.

Raspberry and Fig Brûlées

Serves 4

Working (and total) time: about 10 minutes

Calories 116, Protein 1g, Cholesterol 5mg, Total fat 3g, Saturated fat 2g, Sodium 11 mg

125 g/4 oz *fresh or frozen whole raspberries, thawed*
2 *ripe figs, quartered, thinly sliced*
lengthwise
4 tbsp *soured cream*
4 tbsp *light brown sugar*

Preheat the grill. Divide the raspberries evenly among four 12.5 cl (4 fl oz) ramekins. Arrange one quarter of the fig slices in each ramekin, overlapping the slices as necessary to fit them in. Spread 1 tablespoon of the soured cream over the fig slices in each ramekin, then top each layer of soured cream with 1 tablespoon of the brown sugar rubbed through a sieve. Set the ramekins on a baking sheet and grill them until the brown sugar melts and the soured cream bubbles—1 to 2 minutes. Serve immediately.

Baked Apples
Filled with Grapes

Serves 8

Working tirme: about 50 minutes

Total time: about 1 hour and 40 minutes

Calories 165, Protein 1g, Cholesterol 11mg, Total fat 5g, Saturated fat 3g, Sodium 5mg

8 *tart apples, cored*
¾ litre/1¼ pints *Gewürztztraminer or Riesling*
325 g/11 oz *seedless grapes picked over*
½ tsp *ground mace*
45 g/1½ oz *unsalted butter*

Preheat the oven to 200°C (400°F or Mark 6).

With a paring knife, cut a ring of semicircles in the skin at the top of each apple; as the apples bake, the semicircles will 'blossom' in a floral pattern. Stand the apples upright in a 5 cm (2 inch) deep baking dish and pour 12.5 cl (4 fl oz) of the wine over them. Put the apples into the oven and bake them for 30 minutes.

While the apples are baking, boil the remaining wine in a saucepan over medium-high heat until only about ¼ litre (8 fl oz) remains. Stir the grapes and mace into the wine, then reduce the heat, and simmer the mixture for 30 seconds. With a slotted spoon, remove the grapes from their cooking liquid and set them aside; reserve the liquid.

Spoon the grapes into the apples. Cut the butter into eight pieces and dot each apple with one piece of the butter. Pour the reduced wine over all and return the dish to the oven. Bake the apples until they are tender when pierced with the tip of a knife—15 to 30 minutes more.

To serve, transfer the apples to individual plates. If necessary, use a knife to open up the 'flower petals' you carved in the top of the apples.

Champagne Jelly with Grapes

Serves 6

Working time: about 20 minutes

Total time: about 4 hours (includes chilling)

Calories 185, Protein 3g, Cholesterol 0mg, Total fat 0g,
Saturated fat 0g, Sodium 8mg

750 g/1¹/₂ lb *seedless grapes, stemmed and*
washed

5 tsp *powdered gelatine*

4 tbsp *sugar*

¹/₂ litre/16 fl oz *chilled dry champagne*

Divide the grapes among six 17.5 cl (6 fl oz) moulds;
the grapes should fill each mould no more than three
quarters full. (Alternatively, put all the grapes in a single 1.5 litre/2¹/₂ pint mould.) Refrigerate the moulds.

Pour ¹/₄ litre (8 fl oz) of water into the top of a double
boiler set over simmering water. Sprinkle in the gelatine and heat the mixture, stirring occasionally, until
the gelatine dissolves. Add the sugar and stir until it
too dissolves. Remove the gelatine mixture from the
heat and pour it into a small bowl.

Set the small bowl in a larger bowl filled with ice.
Stir the gelatine mixture until it has cooled to room
temperature. Immediately add the champagne, pouring it against the inside of the bowl to preserve as
many bubbles as possible. With a spoon, gently blend
the champagne into the gelatine mixture. Ladle the
champagne-gelatine mixture into the moulds; spoon
the foam that rises to the top back into the bowl. Repeat the ladling and spooning process until the moulds
are filled to their brims and all the grapes are covered
by the liquid. Freeze the moulds for 30 minutes, then
chill them for at least 3 hours.

At serving time, dip the bottom of a mould in hot
water for 3 seconds; run a knife around the inside of
the mould to break the suction, then invert a chilled
plate on top, and turn both over together. Lift away
the mould. (If the dessert does not unmould, hold the
mould firmly on the plate and give them a brisk shake.)
Repeat the process to unmould the other desserts and
serve them immediately.

Strawberries and Melon in Fruit Jelly

Serves 6

Working time: about 30 minutes

Total time: about 2 hours (includes chilling)

Calories 11 5, Protein 3g, Cholesterol 0mg, Total fat 1g, Saturated fat 0g, Sodium 12mg

---

2½ tsp	powdered gelatine
12.5 c/¼ fl oz	fresh orange juice
4 tbsp	unsweetened white grape juice
1 tbsp	fresh lime juice
2 tbsp	caster sugar
1	melon, halved and seeded
75 g/2½ oz	strawberries
1	kiwi fruit, peeled, thinly sliced crosswise
	Strawberry sauce
150 g/5 oz	strawberries
1 tbsp	caster sugar
½ tbsp	fresh lime juice

Put 3 tablespoons of water into a small bowl; sprinkle in the gelatine and let it stand until it has absorbed all the water and is transparent—about 5 minutes. Combine the orange juice, grapefruit juice, grape juice, the tablespoon of lime juice and the 2 tablespoons of sugar in a saucepan; bring the mixture to the boil, then immediately remove the pan from the heat. Add the gela-

tine mixture to the pan and stir until the gelatine is completely dissolved. Chill the fruit-jelly liquid just until it is syrupy—about 30 minutes—then keep it at room temperature.

With a melon baller, scoop out the melon flesh. Put three or four melon balls in a single layer into each of six 12.5 cl (4 fl oz) ramekins. Pour enough of the fruit jelly mixture into each ramekin to barely cover the melon balls. Chill the ramekins until the jelly sets—about 20 minutes. Slice the 75 g (2½ oz) of strawberries in half lengthwise. Arrange some of the strawberry halves, their cut sides facing out and their stem ends up, round the edge of each ramekin. Fill the ramekins with melon balls, then pour in enough of the remaining mixture to cover the fruit. Chill the ramekins until this layer of jelly sets—at least 1 hour.

To make the strawberry sauce, purée the strawberries with the sugar and lime juice in a food processor or blender. Cover the sauce and chill it.

When the jelly is set, run the tip of a knife round the inside edge of each ramekin. Invert a chilled dessert plate over a ramekin, then turn them both over together and lift away the ramekin. Repeat the process to unmould the other desserts. Pour some of the strawberry sauce round each portion; garnish the desserts with the kiwi slices and the remaining melon balls.

Glazed Fruit Tartlets

Makes 16 tartlets
Working time: about 1 hour
Total time: about 1 hour and 30 minutes
Per tartlet: Calories 120, Protein 3g, Cholesterol 5mg,
Total fat 4g, Saturated fat 2g, Sodium 110mg

140 g/5 oz	*sifted plain flour*
30 g/1 oz	*cold unsalted butter*
15 g/¹/₂ oz	*polyunsaturated margarine*
¹/₂ tsp	salt
2 tbsp	*caster sugar*
¹/₂ tsp	*pure vanilla extract*
2	*ripe nectarines*
300 g/10 oz	*redcurrant jelly or apricot jam*
125 g/4 oz	*fresh raspberries*

Cream filling

175 g/6 oz	*low-fat cottage cheese*
1	*lemon, grated rind only*
2 tbsp	*caster sugar*

Preheat the oven to 200°C (400°F or Mark 6).

To prepare the dough, put the flour, butter, margarine, salt and sugar into a food processor and blend just long enough to produce a fine-meal texture. Alternatively, put the ingredients in a bowl and use a pastry blender or two knives. Add the vanilla extract and 2 tablespoons of water, and continue blending until the mixture forms a ball. Shape the dough into a log about 20 cm (8 inches) long, then wrap it in plastic film, and chill it while you make the filling.

For the filling, purée the cottage cheese in the food processor or blender so that the curd is no longer visible, then blend in the lemon rind and the 2 tablespoons of sugar. Refrigerate the filling.

To form the tartlet shells, divide the dough into 16 equal pieces. Press each piece of dough into a fluted 10 by 5 cm (4 by 2 inch) boat-shaped tartlet tin or a fluted 6 cm (2¹/₂ inch) round tartlet tin (opposite page). Freeze the tartlet shells for 10 minutes. Set the shells on a baking sheet and bake them until their edges start to brown—6 to 8 minutes. Leave the tartlet shells in their tins to cool to room temperature.

Halve the nectarines lengthwise, discarding the stones, then thinly slice the nectarine halves. Melt the jelly or jam in a small saucepan over medium heat, stirring often to prevent sticking. If using jam, sieve it. Allow the mixture to cool slightly; it should be thick enough to coat the fruit.

To assemble the desserts, first remove the tartlet shells from the tins, then spread about 2 teaspoons of the chilled filling inside each shell. Arrange the nectarine slices and raspberries on top of the filling. Brush the fruit lightly with the warm jelly. If the jelly cools to room temperature, reheat it, stirring constantly, until it is thin enough to spread.

Lining Tartlet Moulds with Dough

1 FILLING THE MOULD. After dividing the dough into 16 equal pieces, as called for in the recipe, press one of the pieces into a tartlet mould and spread it across the bottom with your fingers.

2 FORMING THE FLUTED EDGE. Gently force the dough up the fluted sides of the mould, using your fingers, with your thumb, press back down any dough that rises above the top edge of the rim.

Gingery Peach and Almond Tartlets

Serves 10

Working time: about 45 minutes
Total time: about 1 hour and 30 minutes
Calories 150, Protein 3g, Cholesterol 60mg, Total fat 6g,
Saturated fat 1g, Sodium 35mg

5	firm but ripe peaches
75 g/2¹/₂ oz	blanched almonds
4 tbsp	plain flour
¹/₂ tsp	baking powder
¹/₂ tbsp	finely chopped fresh ginger root
100 g/3¹/₂ oz	caster sugar
2	eggs
15 g/¹/₂ oz	unsalted butter, softened

Blanch the peaches in boiling water until their skins loosen—30 seconds to 1 minute. Peel the peaches, then cut them in half, discarding the stones.

Preheat the oven to 170°C (325°F or Mark 3).

Put the almonds, flour, baking powder, ginger and sugar into a food processor or a blender; blend the mixture until the nuts are very finely chopped. Add the eggs and butter, and process them just long enough to blend them in.

Slice one of the peach halves lengthwise and arrange the slices in a lightly oiled 10 cm (4 inch) tartlet tin. Cut and arrange the remaining peach halves the same way. Spoon the almond mixture over the peaches and bake the tartlets until they are lightly browned—30 to 40 minutes.

Let the tartlets cool on a wire rack, then remove them from the tins and serve.

EDITOR'S NOTE: These tartlets may be made in a muffin tin.

42

Cornmeal Tartlets with Tapioca-Blueberry Filling

Serves 8

Working time: about 20 minutes

Total time: about 1 hour and 30 minutes

Calories 273, Protein 3g, Cholesterol 7mg, Total fat 6g,
Saturated fat 2g, Sodium 170mg

175 g/6 oz	*plain flour*
60 g/2 oz	*cornmeal*
60 g/2 oz	*icing sugar*
1/2 tsp	*salt*
1 tbsp	*cornflour*
30 g/1 oz	*cold unsalted butter, cut into 4 pieces*
30 g/1 oz	*cold polyunsaturated margarine, cut into 4 pieces*

Tapioca-blueberry filling

600 g/1 1/4 lb	*fresh blueberries, picked over and stemmed, or frozen blueberries, thawed*
100 g/3 1/2 oz	*caster sugar*
1 tbsp	*fresh lemon juice*
2 tsp	*grated lemon rind*
1 tbsp	*tapioca*

To prepare the tartlet dough, combine the flour, cornmeal, icing sugar, salt and cornflour in a food processor or a bowl. If you are using a food processor, add the butter and margarine, and cut them into the dry ingredients with several short bursts. With the motor running, pour in 2 tablespoons of cold water in a thin, steady stream, and blend the dough just until it forms a ball. If the dough is too dry and crumbly, blend in up to 1 tablespoon more of water. If you are making the dough in a bowl, use two knives to cut the butter and margarine into the dry ingredients, then incorporate the water with a wooden spoon or your hands. Encase the dough in plastic film and refrigerate it for 20 minutes.

Scatter several tablespoons of cornmeal over a clean work surface and roll out the dough to a thickness of about 3 mm (1/8 inch). Alternatively, place the dough between two sheets of greaseproof paper and roll it out. With a biscuit cutter, cut the dough into rounds about 11 cm (4 1/2 inches) in diameter. Use the rounds to line eight 7.5 cm (3 inch) tartlet moulds. Chill the moulds in the freezer for at least 10 minutes. While the moulds are chilling, preheat the oven to 200°C (400°F or Mark 6).

Bake the tartlet shells until they have browned and are crisp—20 to 25 minutes. Remove them from the moulds and cool them on a cake rack.

To prepare the tartlet filling, mix together the blueberries, sugar, lemon juice and lemon rind in a saucepan. Bring the mixture to the boil over medium heat, then continue cooking it until the berries have burst and there is about 1/4 litre (8 fl oz) of juice in the pan—5 to 7 minutes. Stir in the tapioca. Cook the filling, stirring frequently, until it boils and thickens slightly about 10 minutes more. Set the filling aside to cool.

Spoon the cooled filling into the tartlet shells and let them stand for 10 minutes before serving.

Freezing Sorbets and Ice Creams

Frozen desserts count among everyone's favourites. Three different methods for preparing them are examined below. For efficiency, make sure that the dessert mixture is well chilled before you freeze it.

Hand-whisking method

This basic procedure involves placing the dessert mixture in a freezer, then whisking it from time to time as it firms up to break the ice crystals and aerate the mixture. Before starting, turn your freezer to its coldest setting. Use as large a nonreactive metal bowl as will fit into the freezer, or resort to metal ice-cube trays. (Vessels made of glass, a poor conductor of heat, will retard the freezing process.) Place the bowl containing the dessert in the freezer. When a ring of crystals about 1 cm (¹/₂ inch) wide has formed round the outside edge of the mixture, usually after 1 to 2 hours, whisk the mixture. Return the bowl to the freezer and allow another ring of crystals to form before whisking the mixture again. Repeat the whisking a few more times until the dessert is frozen through. After the final whisking, allow the dessert to freeze an additional 15 minutes, then serve it.

Food processor method

This fast and easy method utilizes a food processor once the dessert mixture has set. Freeze the mixture in a non-reactive metal bowl; when the dessert has solidified—the centre may still be soft—break it into chunks and place them in a food processor. (Return the empty bowl to the freezer; you will need it later.) Process the frozen chunks until the dessert has a smooth consistency; be careful not to over-process it or it will melt. Return the dessert to the chilled bowl and let it sit in the freezer—a process that cooks call 'ripening'—for another 15 minutes until it firms up.

Frozen desserts consisting only of fruit juice and a moderate amount of sugar or those containing alcohol will melt faster than those made with fruit purée, a high amount of sugar, egg white, milk or yoghurt. They should be broken into chunks, then processed quickly to break down the crystals without melting. Sorbets prepared according to the food processor method will keep, covered, for several days in the freezer; to restore their consistency, however, they will probably need reprocessing followed by 15 minutes in the freezer.

Churning method

The old-fashioned ice cream maker that demanded half an hour or more of laborious hand-cranking is quickly being replaced by electric and other convenience models, some containing coolants. In using them, be sure to follow the manufacturer's instructions carefully.

Blackberry Sorbet

Serves 6
Working time about 10 minutes
Total time: 1 to 3 hours, depending on freezing method
Calories 225, Protein 1g, Cholesterol 0mg, Total fat 0g, Saturated fat 0g, Sodium 7mg

650 g/1¹/₄ lb	fresh blackberries, picked over or frozen blackberries, thawed
250 g/8 oz	caster sugar
1 tbsp	fresh lemon juice

Purée all but 90 g (3 oz) of the blackberries in a food processor or blender. Strain the purée through a fine sieve into a bowl. Discard any solids remaining in the sieve. Add the sugar and lemon juice to the purée, then stir the mixture until the sugar has dissolved.

Freeze the sorbet, using one of the methods described on the left. Just before serving, garnish the sorbet with the reserved blackberries

EDITOR'S NOTE: If you prefer the sorbet slightly tart, reduce the amount of sugar to 175 g (6 oz).

44

Apple Sorbet
with Candied Almonds

Serves 8

Working time: about 50 minutes

Total time: 1 to 3 hours, depending on freezing method

Calories 250, Protein 1g, Cholesterol 0mg, Total fat 2g,
Saturated fat 0g, Sodium 2mg

10	*tart green apples*
5	*lemons, juice only*
330 g/11 oz	*caster sugar*
30 g/1 oz	*slivered almonds*
1 tbsp	*brown sugar*

Cut off and discard the top quarter of one of the apples. Using a melon baller or spoon, scoop the flesh, core and seeds from the apple, leaving a 5 mm (¹/₂ inch) thick wall. Reserve the flesh; discard the core and seeds. Sprinkle the inside of the apple and the reserved flesh with some of the lemon juice. Repeat the process with all but two of the remaining apples, then freeze the hollowed apples. Peel, seed and chop the two remaining apples, and add them to the reserved flesh.

Put ¹/₂ litre (16 fl oz) of water, 200 g (7 oz) of the sugar and about half of the remaining lemon juice in a

saucepan. Bring the liquid to the boil, reduce the heat to medium, and simmer for 3 minutes. Add the reserved apple flesh and simmer it until it is tender—3 to 4 minutes. With a slotted spoon, transfer the cooked apple flesh to a food processor or blender. Discard the poaching liquid. Purée the apple; put ¹/₂ litre (16 fl oz) of the purée into a bowl and allow it to cool. If any purée is left over, reserve it for another use.

Stir the remaining lemon juice and the remaining sugar into the apple purée. Freeze the mixture, using one of the methods on the opposite page.

While the sorbet is freezing, put the slivered almonds in a small, heavy frying pan over medium heat. Toast the almonds, stirring constantly, until they turn golden-brown—about 5 minutes. Stir in the brown sugar, increase the heat to high, and cook the almonds until they are coated with melted sugar— about 1 minute more. Set the almonds aside.

When the sorbet is firm, scoop or spoon it into the prepared apple cups, then sprinkle some of the candied almonds over each apple Keep the apples in the freezer until they are served.

EDITOR'S NOTE: These sorbets are best consumed within 24 hours of their preparation.

Lemon Cups

Serves 8

Working time: about 30 minutes
Total time: 1 to 3 hours, depending on freezing method
Calories 50, Protein 0g, Cholesterol 0mg, Total fat 0g,
Saturated fat 0g, Sodium 0mg

4 lemons, plus ¹/₂ tsp grated lemon rind
00 g/3¹/₂ oz caster sugar
16 citrus leaves or fresh mint leaves
(optional)

alve the lemons lengthwise, cutting the rind in a
gzag pattern. Remove the pulp and seeds from the
alves with a melon baller or a small, sturdy spoon.
ansfer the pulp to a sieve set over a bowl, and press
own on it with the bottom of a ladle or the back of a
wooden spoon to extract all the juice. Discard the pulp
nd seeds and reserve the juice. Lightly pare the bot-
om of each lemon shell to stabilize it. Freeze the lemon
alves.

Strain 12.5 cl (4 fl oz) of the lemon juice into a bowl.
Any excess juice may be reserved for another use.)
Whisk 35 cl (12 fl oz) of water, the grated rind and the
ugar into the strained lemon juice, stirring until the
ugar has dissolved. Freeze the sorbet, using one of
he methods described on page 44.

When the sorbet is firm, spoon or pipe it into the
emon halves and return them to the freezer. If you
ke, garnish each lemon cup with two of the citrus or
hint leaves before serving.

Lime Cups

Serves 8

Working time: about 30 minutes
Total time: 1 to 3 hours, depending on freezing method
Calories 50, Protein 0g, Cholesterol 0mg, Total fat 0g,
Saturated fat 0g, Sodium 0mg

8 limes, plus 1 tsp grated lime rind
2 tbsp fresh lemon juice
100 g/3¹/₂ oz caster sugar
1 egg white (optional)
8 citrus leaves or fresh mint leaves
(optional)

Cut each lime in half lengthwise. Remove the pulp
from the shells with a melon baller or a small spoon.
Transfer the pulp to a sieve set over a bowl, and press
down on the pulp with the bottom of a ladle or the
back of a wooden spoon to extract all the juice. Discard the pulp and seeds, and reserve the juice. Lightly
pare the bottom of the shells to stabilize them. Freeze
the lime shells.

Strain 6 tablespoons of the lime juice into a bowl.
(Any extra juice may be reserved for another use.)
Whisk in the lemon juice, 35 cl (12 fl oz) water, the
lime rind, sugar and egg white, and stir until the sugar
has dissolved. Freeze the sorbet, using one of the
methods described on page 44.

When the sorbet is firm, pipe or spoon it into the
lime shells and return them to the freezer. If you like,
garnish each lime shell with a citrus or mint leaf.

EDITOR'S NOTE: The egg white called for here keeps the
sorbet from freezing too hard, making it easier to pipe. An
egg white may likewise be added to any citrus sorbet in
this section.

Kiwi Sorbet

Serves 4
Working time: about 15 minutes
Total time: 1 to 3 hours, depending on freezing method
Calories 190, Protein 2g, Cholesterol 0mg, Total fat 1g, Saturated fat 0g, Sodium 8mg

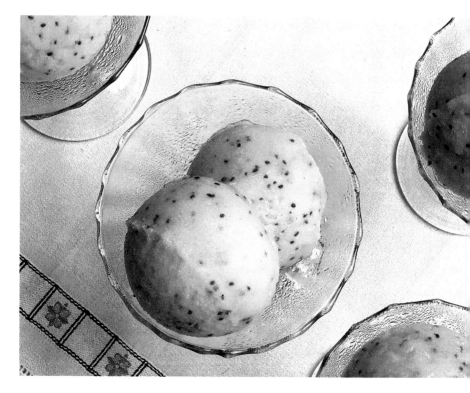

8 *kiwi fruits*
2 tbsp *fresh lemon juice*
100 g/3¹/₂ oz *caster sugar*

Cut a thin slice from both ends of a kiwi fruit. Stand the fruit on a cutting board. Remove the rest of the skin by slicing vertical strips from the sides of the fruit, taking care not to cut off too much of the flesh. Peel the remaining kiwis the same way.

Quarter each kiwi fruit and put the pieces into a food processor or a blender. Process the kiwis just long enough to purée them without cracking their seeds. Add the lemon juice and sugar, and blend them in.

Freeze the mixture, using one of the methods on page 44. Serve the kiwi sorbet in scoops.

Orange and Passion Fruit Cups

Serves 8

Working time: about 30 minutes
Total time: 1 to 3 hours, depending on freezing method
Calories 160, Protein 1g, Cholesterol 0mg, Total fat 0g,
Saturated fat 0g, Sodium 4mg

8 *large oranges (about 2 kg/4 lb)*
4 *passion fruit*
200 g/7 oz *caster sugar*

Halve the oranges crosswise, cutting the rind in a zigzag pattern as demonstrated below. Remove the pulp and seeds from the halves with a melon baller or a small sturdy spoon. Transfer the pulp to a sieve set over a bowl, and press down on the pulp with the bottom of a ladle or the back of a wooden spoon to extract all the juice. Discard the pulp and seeds. Pour 1 litre (1³/₄ pints) of the orange juice into a bowl. With a small spoon, scrape any remaining pulp from eight of the orange halves to form orange cups. Freeze these cups; discard the remaining orange shells.

Cut the tops off the passion fruit. Scoop out the pulp and seeds and purée them in a food processor or a blender. Strain the purée into the bowl with the orange juice, then whisk in the sugar. Freeze the mixture, using one of the techniques described on page 44.

When the sorbet is firm, scoop or spoon it into the frozen orange cups. Return the cups to the freezer for about 30 minutes before serving them.

EDITOR'S NOTE: An equally delicious sorbet results when tangerine juice replaces the orange juice. The dish may also be prepared without the passion fruit, in which case 2 tablespoons of fresh lemon juice should be used in their stead.

A Zigzag Cut for Fruit Cups

1 FORMING A FLAT BOTTOM. Holding a citrus fruit (here, an orange) steady, use a small, stainless steel knife to cut a thin slice from its bottom so that the fruit will sit flat when served. (For a lemon, which should be halved lengthwise for greater holding capacity, cut thin slices from two opposite sides to create bases)

2 CUTTING ROUND THE FRUIT. Stand the orange on its flat end. Insert the knife in to the midsection at a slant, cutting to the core. Withdraw the knife and make a vertical incision adjacent to the first cut. Alternate slanted and vertical cuts round the orange until the cuts meet.

3 SEPARATING THE BOTTOM HALVES. To separate the halves, lift off the top; if the halves stick, twist the top and bottom in opposite directions to separate the pieces. Remove the pulp and juice as indicated in the recipe.

Cranberry Sorbet

Serves 8
Working time: about 15 minutes
Total time: 1 to 3 hours depending on freezing method
Calories 165, Protein 0g, Cholesterol 0mg, Total fat 0g, Saturated fat 0g, Sodium 1mg

350 g/12 oz *fresh or frozen cranberries*
300 g/10 oz *caster sugar*
2 tbsp *fresh lemon juice*
1 *kiwi fruit (optional), peeled and thinly sliced*

Put the cranberries into a saucepan with 60 cl (1 pint) of water. Bring the mixture to a simmer and cook it just until the cranberries pop—about 2 minutes. Pass the mixture through a sieve, rubbing the cranberries through with the back of a wooden spoon. Stir in the sugar and lemon juice, then freeze the mixture as described on page 44.

Serve the sorbet in scoops; if you like, garnish each portion with the kiwi slices.

Plum and Red Wine Sorbet with Raisin Sauce

Serves 10

Working time: about 25 minutes
Total time: about 1 day

Calories 180, Protein 1g, Cholesterol 0mg, Total fat 0g,
Saturated fat 0g, Sodium 3mg

60 cl/1 pint	*red wine*
250 g/8 oz	*sugar*
500 g/1 lb	*ripe red plums, quartered and stoned, two of the quarters sliced for garnish*
2 tbsp	*fresh lemon juice*
45 g/1½ oz	*raisins*

Combine ½ litre (16 fl oz) of the wine with the sugar in a heavy-bottomed saucepan over medium heat. Bring the mixture to the boil, stirring to dissolve the sugar. When the liquid reaches the boil, reduce the heat, cover the pan, and simmer the syrup for 2 minutes. Stir in the plum quarters; as soon as the syrup returns to a simmer, cover the pan again and cook the plums for 4 minutes more. Strain 12.5 cl (4 fl oz) of the syrup into a small bowl and set it aside for the sauce.

To prepare the sorbet, first purée the plum-wine mixture in a blender or food processor. Blend in the

remaining wine and the lemon juice. Let the mixture cool to room temperature, then chill it.

Using one of the methods described on page 44, freeze the sorbet mixture until it is firm but not hard. Transfer the frozen sorbet to a metal mould or bowl. Rap the bottom of the mould or bowl on the counter once or twice to collapse any large air bubbles. Cover the container tightly with plastic film and freeze the sorbet overnight.

To prepare the sauce, combine the reserved 12.5 cl (4 fl oz) of syrup with the raisins and sultanas in a small, heavy-bottomed saucepan. Quickly bring the mixture to the boil, then immediately remove the pan from the heat. Let the sauce cool to room temperature before refrigerating it; the dried fruit will plump up.

Shortly before serving time, unmould the sorbet. Dip the bottom of the mould in hot water for 15 seconds; invert a chilled platter on top and turn both over together. If the dessert does not unmould, wrap it in a towel that has been soaked in hot water. After 15 seconds, remove the towel and lift the mould away. Garnish the sorbet with the reserved plum slices, then cut the sorbet into wedges with a cake slice that has been dipped into hot water. Serve some of the raisin sauce with each portion.

Mint Julep Ice

Serves 8

Working time: about 15 minutes

Total time: 1 to 3 hours, depending on freezing method

Calories 180, Protein 0g, Cholesterol 0mg, Total fat 0g,
Saturated fat 0g, Sodium 3mg

250 g/8 oz *caster sugar*
60 g/2 oz *fresh mint leaves plus 2 tbsp chopped fresh mint*
17.5 cl/6 fl oz *bourbon*
2 *lemons, juice only*
8 *mint sprigs for garnish*

n a heavy-bottomed saucepan, combine the sugar, ³/ litre (1¼ pints) of water and the mint leaves. Bring the mixture to the boil over medium heat, stirring to dissolve the sugar. When the mint syrup reaches the boil, cover the pan and boil the syrup for 1 minute. Pour the syrup through a fine sieve into a medium bowl. Allow the syrup to cool to room temperature and then chill it in the refrigerator for about 30 minutes.

When the syrup is cold, combine the 2 tablespoons of chopped mint, the bourbon and the lemon juice in a small bowl. Stir the bourbon mixture into the syrup; freeze the mint julep ice until it is firm, using one of the methods described on page 44.

To serve, scoop the ice into eight sorbet dishes or mint julep cups. Garnish each serving with a sprig of mint.

Gewürztraminer Sorbet with Frosted Grapes

THE WHITE ALSATIAN WINE CALLED FOR IN THIS RECIPE PRODUCES A FULL FLAVOURED SORBET.

Serves 6

Working time: about 10 minutes

Total time: 1 to 3 hours, depending on freezing method

Calories 225, Protein 1g, Cholesterol 0mg, Total fat 0g,
Saturated fat 0g, Sodium 11mg

1 *egg white*
80 g/2½ oz *seedless green grapes*
80 g/2½ oz *seedless red grapes*
250 g/8 oz *caster sugar*
35 cl/12 fl oz *Gewürztraminer or Riesling wine*

Whisk together the egg white and ½ tablespoon of water in a bowl. Add all the grapes and stir to coat them with the egg white mixture.

Spread the sugar on a dinner plate. Lift a grape from the egg white and roll it in the sugar, coating it with a generous layer of sugar. Transfer the frosted grape to a clean plate. Coat the remaining grapes the same way, transferring each one to the plate as you finish. To solidify the frosting, let the grapes stand at room temperature while you make the sorbet.

Put ½ litre (16 fl oz) of water and the wine into a bowl, then whisk in the sugar left on the plate. Freeze the sorbet, using one of the methods described on page 44.

Serve the sorbet in scoops, garnishing each portion with a few frosted grapes.

Gin and Pink Grapefruit Sorbet

Serves 6
Working time: about 15 minutes
Total time: 1 to 3 hours, depending on freezing method
Calories 215, Protein 1g, Cholesterol 0mg, Total fat 0g, Saturated fat 0g, Sodium 2mg

1 litre/1³/₄ pints *fresh pink grapefruit juice*
200 g *caster sugar*
4 tbsp *gin*
1 tbsp *grenadine (optional)*

Combine the grapefruit juice, sugar, gin and grenadine,
If you are using it, in a bowl; stir to dissolve the sugar.
Freeze the mixture, using one of the methods described on page 44. If you like, present scoops of the
sorbet in tulipes.

Strawberry and Champagne Sorbet

THE SUCCESS OF THIS RECIPE DEPENDS PARTLY UPON STARTING OUT
WITH CHILLED STRAWBERRIES AND CHAMPAGNE.

Serves 6

Working time: about 15 minutes

Total time: 1 to 2 hours, depending on freezing method

Calories 170, Protein 0g, Cholesterol 0mg, Total fat 0g,
Saturated fat 0g, Sodium 4mg

---

350 g/12 oz *hulled strawberries, quartered and chilled*
150 g/5 oz *caster sugar*
2 tbsp *fresh lemon juice*
¹/₂ litre/16 fl oz *chilled dry champagne*
6 *strawberries for garnish*

Put the strawberry quarters, sugar and lemon juice in a food processor or blender; process the mixture briefly so that the berries are finely chopped—not puréed. Add the champagne, pouring it slowly against the inside of the bowl to keep it from frothing. Blend quickly to retain as much effervescence as possible, then freeze the mixture, using one of the methods described on page 44.

Scoop the sorbet into dessert glasses. If you like, garnish each portion with a strawberry and serve with a glass of chilled champagne.

55

Frozen Peach Yoghurt

Serves 6

Working time: about 15 minutes
Total time: 1 to 3 hours, depending on freezing method
Calories 145, Protein 5g, Cholesterol 3mg, Total fat 1g,
Saturated fat 1g, Sodium 60mg

750 g/1¹/₂ lb	*ripe peaches*
2 tbsp	*fresh lemon juice, plus 1 tsp grated lemon rind*
1 tbsp	*grated orange rind*
35 cl/12 fl oz	*plain low-fat yoghurt*
2	*egg whites*
125 g/4 oz	*honey*
3 tbsp	*brandy (optional)*

Leaving the peaches unpeeled, halve and stone them. Set one of the peach halves aside. Put the remaining peach halves into a food processor or a blender, together with the lemon juice, lemon rind and orange rind; purée the mixture. Add the yoghurt, the egg whites, the honey, and the brandy if you are using it, and blend the mixture for 5 seconds

Freeze the mixture, following one of the techniques described on page 44.

Before serving, thinly slice the reserved peach half. Scoop the frozen yoghurt into dessert glasses or dishes and garnish with the peach slices.

Frozen Vanilla Yoghurt

Serves 4

Working time: about 10 minutes
Total time: 1 to 3 hours, depending on freezing method
Calories 165, Protein 9g, Cholesterol 9mg, Total fat 2g,
Saturated fat 2g, Sodium 125mg

12.5 cl/4 fl oz	*semi-skimmed milk*
5 cm/2 inch	*length of vanilla pod, or I tsp vanilla extract*
¹/₂ litre	*plain low-fat yoghurt*
2	*egg whites*
6 tbsp	*caster sugar*

If you are using the vanilla pod, warm the milk in a saucepan over low heat. Split the vanilla pod lengthwise and add it to the milk. Remove the pan from the heat and let the vanilla pod steep until the milk has cooled to room temperature—about 15 minutes.

Remove the pod from the milk and scrape the seeds inside it into the milk. If you are using vanilla extract, simply combine it with the unheated milk.

Whisk the yoghurt, egg whites and sugar into the milk. Freeze the mixture using one of the methods desribed on page 44.

Frozen Raspberry Yoghurt

Serves 6

Working time about 15 minutes
Total time: 1 to 3 hours, depending on freezing method
Calories 140, Protein 5g, Cholesterol 5mg, Total fat 1g,
Saturated fat 1g, Sodium 70mg

300 g/10 oz	*fresh or frozen raspberries, thawed*
¹/₂ litre	*plain low-fat yoghurt*
100 g/3¹/₂ oz	*caster sugar*
2	*egg whites*
4 tbsp	*creme de cassis (optional)*

Purée the raspberries in a food processor or a blender. Then, to remove the raspberry seeds, pass the purée through a fine sieve into a bowl; use a spatula to force the purée through the wire mesh. Combine the purée with the yoghurt and sugar, whisk in the egg whites, then freeze the mixture using one of the methods described on page 44.

Pass the creme de cassis separately so that each diner can pour a little over the yoghurt

EDITOR'S NOTE: If desired, two yoghurts can be swirled together. Make frozen vanilla yoghurt (recipe above). Spoon the frozen raspberry yoghurt inside a piping bag, keeping it to one side; spoon the frozen vanilla yoghurt on top of the raspberry yoghurt, filling the otherside of the bag. Pipe out the two yoghurts together in a mounting spiral.

Frozen Banana Yoghurt with Streusel Crumbs

Serves 8

Working time: about 15 minutes

Total time: 1 to 3 hours, depending on freezing method

Calories 190, Protein 6g, Cholesterol 8mg, Total fat 3g, Saturated fat 2g, Sodium 100mg

---

350 g/12 oz	*ripe bananas*
2 tbsp	*fresh lemon juice*
1/2 litre/16 fl oz	*plain low-fat yoghurt*
2	*egg whites, at room temperature*
6 tbsp	*caster sugar*
3	*slices wholemeal bread*
15 g/1/2 oz	*unsalted butter*
4 tbsp	*light brown sugar*
1 tbsp	*finely chopped walnuts*

Purée the bananas and lemon juice in a food processor or a blender. Add the yoghurt, egg whites and caster sugar, and blend the mixture for 5 seconds.

Freeze the yoghurt mixture, using one of the methods described on page 44.

While the yoghurt mixture is freezing, make the streusel: preheat the oven to 170°C (325°F or Mark 3). Tear each slice of bread into three or four pieces; put the bread pieces in a food processor or a blender and process them until they are reduced to fine crumbs. Spread the crumbs in a baking tin and bake them, stirring once or twice to ensure even cooking, until they are crisp—about 15 minutes. Cut the butter into small bits and scatter them over the breadcrumbs. Return the pan to the oven just long enough to melt the butter—about 1 minute. Stir the breadcrumbs to coat them with the butter, then transfer the mixture to a bowl. Stir in the brown sugar and walnuts, and set the mixture aside.

When the yoghurt mixture is nearly frozen—it will still be soft—stir in all but 2 tablespoons of the streusel mixture. Return the yoghurt to the freezer for approximately 15 minutes more to firm it up. Just before serving the yoghurt, sprinkle the reserved streusel over the top.

Iced Apple Mousse Cake with Brandy Snaps

Serves 12

Working time: about 1 hour

Total time: 2¹/₂ to 4 hours, depending on freezing method

Calories 175, Protein 2g, Cholesterol 10mg, Total fat 4g, Saturated fat 2g, Sodium 30mg

1 kg	*crisp eating apples*
4 tbsp	*fresh lemon juice*
¹/₂ tsp	*ground cloves*
¹/₂ tsp	*ground cinnamon*
30 g/1 oz	*unsalted butter*
100 g/3¹/₂ oz	*caster sugar*
6	*egg whites*
12	*tuile brandy snaps*
Apple fans	
2	*crisp eating apples*
2 tsp	*honey*

To make the apple mousse, peel and core the 1 kg (2 lb) of apples, then cut them into 1 cm (¹/₂ inch) chunks. Toss the apples with the lemon juice, cloves and cinnamon.

Melt the butter in a large, heavy frying pan over medium heat. Add the apple mixture and cook it, stirring frequently, for about 10 minutes. Sprinkle in the sugar and continue to cook the mixture stirring often, for 5 minutes more.

Put the apple mixture into a food processor or a blender and process it until it is very smooth, stopping at least once to scrape down the sides. Transfer the mixture to a shallow bowl and whisk in the egg whites. Freeze the mixture, using one of the methods described on page 44.

Preheat the oven to 180°C (350°F or Mark 4).

To prepare the apple fans, peel the remaining two apples and cut them in half lengthwise. Remove the cores, then slice the apple halves thinly, keeping the slices together. Fan out each sliced apple half on a baking sheet. Dribble the honey over the apple fans and bake them until they are tender—about 15 minutes. Allow the fans to cool to room temperature, then refrigerate them.

Transfer the apple mousse to a 23 cm (9 inch) springform tin and freeze it until it is solid—about 1 hour.

To unmould the cake, run a knife round the inside of the tin, then place a hot, damp towel on the bottom for about 10 seconds. Invert a plate on the cake; turn both cake and plate over together. Remove the sides of the tin, and smooth the surface of the cake with a long knife or spatula.

Arrange the chilled apple fans on top of the cake; decorate the sides of the cake with the brandy snaps.

Two-Melon Ice with Poppy Seeds and Port Sauce

Serves 8

Working time: about 15 minutes

Total time: 1 to 3 hours, depending on freezing method

Calories 183, Protein 2g, Cholesterol 0mg, Total fat 1g, Saturated fat 0g, Sodium 20mg

Port Sauce

Calories 65, Protein 0g, Cholesterol 0mg, Total fat 0g, Saturated fat 0g, Sodium 2 mg

1	*ripe honeydew melon (about 2.5 kg/5 lb)*
1	*ripe cantaloupe melon (about 1.5 kg/3 lb)*
1 tsp	*poppy seeds*
1/8 tsp	*ground mace*
4 tbsp	*fresh lemon juice*
200 to 275 g/7 to 9 oz	*caster sugar, depending on the sweetness of the melon*

Port Sauce

35 cl/12 fl oz	*ruby port*
2 tbsp	*cornflour*

With a narrow-bladed knife, halve the honeydew melon crosswise, using a zigzag cut to produce a sawtooth pattern in the rind. Remove and discard the seeds. Select the more attractive half of the melon for serving; with a melon baller, scoop from it balls of flesh. Refrigerate the melon balls in a large bowl. Cut some of the flesh from the other melon half and purée it in a food processor or a blender—there should be about ¾ litre (16 fl oz) of purée. If the purée measures less than 1/2 litre (16 fl oz), process more melon flesh, if it measures more, reserve the excess for another use. Refrigerate the purée.

Slice the cantaloupe in half with a simple crosswise cut. Scoop out one half into balls and refrigerate them with the honeydew balls until serving time. Cut the

emaining cantaloupe half into chunks and purée the chunks to produce ¹/₂ litre (16 fl oz) of purée. Stir the cantaloupe and honeydew purées together and chill them.

Discard all the melon shells except the honeydew half you selected for serving. Scrape the inside of the shell clean. Pare a thin slice from the bottom so that the melon will stand upright, then freeze the shell.

Combine the chilled melon purée with the poppy seeds, mace, lemon juice and sugar. Freeze the mixture, using one of the methods described on page 44.

To make the sauce, bring 30 cl (¹/₂ pint) of the port to the boil in a saucepan. Combine the remaining port with the cornflour and stir the mixture into the boiling port. Cook the sauce, stirring constantly, until it thickens—about 1 minute. Allow the sauce to cool to room temperature, then chill it.

Use an ice-cream scoop to fill the frozen honeydew shell with balls of the melon ice. Scatter the chilled melon balls over the top and pass the sauce separately.

Cappuccino Parfaits

Serves 8
Working time: about 35 minutes
Total time: 1 to 3 hours, depending on freezing method
Calories 130, Protein 1g, Cholesterol 11mg, Total fat 3g,
Saturated fat 2g, Sodium 16mg

1	orange, pared rind only
2 tbsp	high-roast instant coffee powder
200 g/7 oz	caster sugar
4 tbsp	double cream
¹/₂ tsp	ground cinnamon
2	egg whites
	cocoa powder

In a heatproof bowl, combine the orange rind, instant coffee powder, 150 g (5 oz) of the sugar and ¹/₂ litre (16 fl oz) of boiling water. Stir to dissolve the sugar, then let the orange rind steep for 10 minutes. Remove the rind and discard it. Using one of the techniques described on page 44, freeze the coffee mixture.

When the mixture is frozen, divide it among eight glass coffee cups or glasses; freeze the containers.

In a small bowl, whip together the cream and cinnamon until soft peaks form; set the mixture aside. In another bowl, beat the egg whites until they can hold soft peaks when the beater is lifted from the bowl. Continue beating, gradually adding the remaining sugar, until the whites are glossy and form stiff peaks. Fold the whipped cream into the egg whites. Fill each of the cups or glasses with some of the egg whitecream mixture. Freeze the parfaits until they are firm—about 30 minutes.

Just before serving the parfaits, dust each one with some cocoa powder.

Frozen Piña Coladas

Serves 8
Working time: about 20 minutes
Total time: about 2 hours and 20 minutes
Calories 125, Protein 3g, Cholesterol 2mg, Total fat 2g,
Saturated fat 1g, Sodium 80mg

75 g/2¹/2 oz *fresh pineapple flesh, chopped*
75 g/2¹/2 oz *peeled banana, chopped*
¹/2 litre/16 fl oz *buttermilk*
100 g/3¹/2 oz *caster sugar*
2 *egg whites*
4 tbsp *dark rum*
3 tbsp *shredded coconut for garnish*

Process the pineapple and the banana in a blender or
a food processor stopping once to scrape down the
sides with a rubber spatula, until every trace of fibre
has disappeared and a smooth purée results—about
1 minute. (There should be approximately ¹/4 litre/8 f
oz of purée.) Blend in the buttermilk, sugar, egg whites
and rum. Freeze the mixture, using one of the methods described on page 44.

Scoop the sorbet into glasses and keep in the freezer
until serving time

To toast the coconut, spread it in a baking tin and
set it in a preheated 180°C (350°F or Mark 4) oven
Toast the coconut, stirring every 5 minutes, until it is
lightly browned—15 to 20 minutes.

Just before serving the desserts, sprinkle some of
the toasted coconut over each one.

Grape Lollies

THESE FROZEN CONFECTIONS ARE FORMED IN A MADELEINE TRAY.

Makes 12
Total time about 1 hour and 20 minutes
Calories 70, Protein 0g, Cholesterol 0mg, Total fat 0g,
Saturated fat 0g, Sodium 2mg

500 g/1 lb seedless green grapes
500 g/1 lb seedless black grapes
5 tbsp caster sugar

Purée the green grapes in a food processor or a blender. Strain the purée through a fine sieve into a small saucepan. Bring the purée to a simmer over medium-high heat, then stir in 2½ tablespoons of the sugar, and remove the pan from the heat. When the mixture has cooled to room temperature, pour it into a 12 space madeleine tray, filling each space to the brim. Reserve the excess purée. Chill the tray in the freezer until the purée has nearly set—about 30 minutes.

Lay the end of a flat ice lolly stick in the centre of each of the six frozen sorbets in the bottom row of the tray; the sticks should overhang the tray's bottom edge. Return the tray to the freezer.

While the tray is chilling, purée the black grapes in a food processor or blender and strain the purée into the saucepan. Bring the purée to a simmer over medium-high heat, then stir in the remaining 2½ tablespoons of sugar, and remove the pan from the heat. Pour the mixture into a bowl and set it aside to cool.

When the green-grape mixture has frozen solid, remove the madeleine tray from the freezer, pop out the sorbets in the top row and brush their flat sides with the reserved green-grape mixture. Set one of the painted sorbets on top of a sorbet that is still in the tray, and press it in place. Repeat the process to form six lollies in all, then return the tray to the freezer for 30 minutes.

When the green-grape lollies have frozen solid, remove them from the tray mould and return them to the freezer. Clean the mould and use it to make six black-grape lollies, using the same method.

EDITOR'S NOTE: Wooden or plastic ice lolly sticks are sold at newsagents and kitchen shops.

Spiced Coffee Ice Cream

Serves 8

Working time: about 15 minutes

Total time: 1 to 3 hours, depending on freezing method

Calories 160, Protein 6g, Cholesterol 15mg, Total fat 5g, Saturated fat 3g, Sodium 70mg

325 g/11 oz	*low-fat ricotta cheese*
12.5 cl/4 fl oz	*plain low-fat yoghurt*
135 g/4¹/₂ oz	*caster sugar*
¹/₄ litre/8 fl oz	*freshly brewed triple strength coffee, strained and chilled*
¹/₂ tsp	*ground cinnamon*
¹/₂ tsp	*ground cardamom, or ¹/₄ tsp grated nutmeg*
¹/₂ tsp	*pure vanilla extract*
30 g/1 oz	*plain chocolate, grated*

Purée the ricotta, yoghurt and sugar in a food processor or a blender, stopping at least once to scrape down the sides, until you have a very smooth purée. Whisk the coffee, cinnamon, cardamom or nutmeg, vanilla and chocolate into the purée. Freeze, using one of the techniques on page 44. If using the food processor method, add the chocolate after processing the mixture.